Just follow the map

How hard can it be?

A cycling misadventure across Britain (Eventually)

Written by

Kevin Pilcher

Dedication

This book is dedicated to Gail, Jodie, Ed & Ralph the cat. Well, they'd all be a bit cross if I didn't after all that they've had to endure (apart from Ralph, he couldn't give a monkey's as long as he's fed)

Introduction

Introduction

This is not the story of an epic adventure across continents, of fighting off wild animals in temperatures either so hot that you could boil a cat or so cold that you could…. Er…. Freeze a dog! Oh no, this is the sorry tale of one, some might say, deluded man and his feeble attempt to pedal his bike across a small part of a very small Island.

That man is me!

My recollections may be like fingerprints on an abandoned handrail, as a certain Mr. Mortimer may have uttered, but every detail, to the best of my limited knowledge, is true and no names have been changed to protect the innocent. Any submissions or views stated are only my own personal observations, but most, if not all should become Government policy as a matter of urgency. Either that or just be accepted as the rantings of, said, deluded man whilst riding his bike.

It's a *"Warts an' all"* tale with plenty of warts believe me. Any alleged funny bits are meant to be just that. Please remember that a joke is just a joke, it's put in to make folk laugh, titter or smile and is not meant to be taken seriously. I don't do offensive humour and I don't do swearing, so this can be read by anyone aged from 9 or under to 90 and beyond.

When Queen penned the lyric in Bohemian Rhapsody *"Any way the wind blows, doesn't really matter to me"* it became obvious that they weren't cyclists because it does matter, oh yes it matters.

I so much wanted to be able to say to folk *"I'm a touring cyclist"*

At least I had a go!

1. *And in the Beginning....*

It started with a heart attack and then became an obsession. In between there was a hip replacement that hasn't entirely worked as I seem to be in as much pain now as I was before the operation, but Hey Ho! That was part of the reason for getting on a bike in the first place.

After I had my slight heart altercation on 14th May 2003 (you never forget the date, believe me) whilst repairing the little old lady next door's fence, I found myself in a bit of a mental state , not to mention the physical trauma that I also went through.

After enduring two weeks in hospital, a stent and enough medication to help keep the pharmaceutical Industry going for many years, I suffered from acute anxiety and depression and required counselling from a brilliant, sensitive and sympathetic lady counsellor (I bet that you're thinking *"what a funny and exciting cycling book this is so far "*) .It was thanks to her and my better (questionable) half Gail and daughter Jodie that I got over the shock of the heart attack eventually. I was only 45 years old after all, although my fitness and dietary habits may have left a lot to be desired.

After some time, both recovering and feeling sorry for myself, I looked at Jodie's mountain bike in the shed. Hmmmm!

By raising up the saddle and putting more upright BMX handlebars on to make it a more comfortable riding position for me, I gave it a bash up and down the road. Some saddle padding and customizing in general followed, and I was away. Despite Jodie being only ten at the time I did actually fit the bike even though I was over six feet tall (The nurse told me that I was only actually five foot seven but what do they know? Her measuring wall was obviously wrong!).

I named the bike *"The Easy Rider"* for absolutely no reason at all.

I started off by cycling from my mum and dad's house along the Royal Military Canal in Hythe Kent, and some days I even managed three miles, but that was only on good days.

As my confidence in my heart improved the only thing that prevented me from cycling too much was my right hip and knackered knees. I had had Perthes Desease in my hip since the age of ten. It's where the hip just wears away and crumbles due to lack of fluids etc. and anybody who has experienced it will know that it can be absolute agony. Still, ne'er mind eh!

It clicked and clunked as I tried to pedal along but it got so bad in 2008 that I had to have an urgent replacement. As luck would have it, I was given one of the last metal on metal joints just before they found that there could be problems with them.

Oh well you've got to laugh, haven't you?

Anyway, as the recovery from my new hip ensued, I attended a Physiotherapy group at the hospital. I absolutely loved using the exercise bike and a chair where you either pushed down or pulled up weights. I was starting to build up my right leg muscles for the first time in many years when the group came to a stop.

I wanted to carry on exercising this way as I was told that as well as being good for my hip and legs, it was also great cardiac exercise for me. What a stroke of luck that I enjoyed cycling. I found myself going out as much as I could. I actually got pain relief from cycling and, as much as possible, it became my physiotherapy and medication instead of prescribed drugs as the problems with my new hip developed.

It was weird. I was finding it increasingly more painful and difficult to walk, sit or stand but it only eased when I was on the bike. My consultant and G.P. agreed and encouraged me to carry on pedalling as it became my only source of relief.

As my cycling ventured further around the area it got me thinking about actually cycling *"Somewhere"*.

2 From little acorns….

My middle daughter, Kerry, told me one day that she was doing a sponsored, supported ride from London to Paris with a friend in a larger group, and as she was obviously passing near to us on route to Dover, Gail and myself drove out to near Faversham to help and to cheer them on, giving encouragement all of the way to the Port.

She completed the 300 mile trip and felt justly proud of her achievement. I was proud of her as well. Then it got me thinking even more. I would like to do a trip myself. I couldn't do one like that though as it was quite costly, far too organized for an ageing old hippy like me (I didn't like helmets for a start and you had to wear one at all times) and I wanted to do mine unsupported, carrying all of my own gear in panniers like a proper cycle tourist. The seed was sown.

My months of criss-crossing the Romney Marsh area and up onto the North Downs (High country) around the villages, some that I knew well like Court At Street, where I was born on a farm and brought up and learned to ride a bike around the farmyard, Aldington, where I first went to school, Lympne, (pronounced Lym) where I was christened and went to village fetes (All *"Darling Buds of May" country),* and some that I didn't know at all, turned into a couple of years.

I was sometimes cycling as much as twenty odd miles on a nice day on my little sturdy, very heavy trusty steed, but the time had come for me to progress on to a newer machine so one day we called into Romney cycles and I immediately spotted a dark green Claud Butler Hybrid touring bike. I Ummed and Ahhed so Gail took control and instructed me to get it, and (not being one to argue) I did. I arranged for them to extend the handlebar height and cable's to enable me a more upright riding position and put in a new back gear cassette to incorporate a *"Granny gear"*. I then fitted a nice padded saddle and named the bike *"Stan"* (From the old TV comedy *"On the buses"* Get it?). I then set the "Easy Rider" aside to enjoy a well earned retirement. I'm quite a softy at heart, and a bit dopey!

The road from Aldington to Court at Street where I spent many happy days cycling along on all of my bikes

Now, astride Stan, a 21 speed hybrid touring bike, I was able to enjoy longer, more comfortable rides, although at first I felt like a dwarf on a penny farthing as I seemed to be, and was, much higher off the ground. Stan had many admiring smiles and comments and I must confess that despite a couple of punctures and broken spokes, I was feeling confident about actually putting a shortish tour together. At the same time I was buying camping gear and various pieces of bike equipment that, in my mind, I would need.

None of your expensive gear, mind. This all came from boot fairs, charity shops or from China, via Ebay. I knew quality when I saw it!

Now all I had to do was to decide where to ride. I had read numerous cycling memoirs ranging from Lands End to John O'Groats, around Britain, around Europe and around the World. Most, if not all, were beyond my means and, possibly, my capabilities (for now).

Also, I realized that this was going to be a solo jaunt as I knew nobody daft enough to join me. To be honest, although a bit daunting and scary, this didn't really bother me as all of my daily cycles had been on my Todd.

I thought that it would be great to cycle from another country and I had dreamt about crossing the River Severn on my bike, so Wales became my hopefully chosen start point. I could cycle home from there. Brilliant!!!! Then it occurred to me that I could do the Kennett & Avon canal towpath, another dream. From Devizes I could make for the South coast somehow and follow the sea home. I could fill in the gaps as I went. The Idea was put to the family and the response wasn't quite what I'd anticipated. Gail said that she thought that I could end up in hospital, Jodie, on the other hand was more confident in my ability. She was sure that I would die! Ralph the cat declined to comment.

I suppose that I could understand their standpoint, to a certain extent anyway. They had both nearly lost me a few years previous due to my little heart misadventure (careless), and during my recovery from that , had seen me suffer from my hippy shoes (Hip Issues! brilliant eh?), and the constant agonies that had spread around my lower spine and groin area. Oh woe is me!

On the other hand, I told them that I needed, wanted to do this as it would be good therapy for me and the alternative, doing nowt but sitting in pain, dreaming didn't bear thinking about. I went on and on about it until they agreed (to shut me up). Jodie even offered to get me to the Welsh border for the start. It was all falling into place now. What could possibly go wrong?

If only I knew!

July 2015 was to be D-Day so I started to get my kit together ready for the "Off". I lost a couple more spokes on Stan's back wheel and one on the front, so after getting them replaced I thought it best to carry a few spares on the trip (Cunning eh?).

I only booked B&B at a pub in the village of Holt near Bradford on Avon, about fifty miles from Chepstow. I thought that I would either find a campsite or B&B as I went after that. To that end I had lists written down and places marked on my many maps, all old Ordnance Survey jobs dating back to The Magna Carta. The one thing that didn't occur to me was that I had never ever camped in my life. Still, I had erected the tent in the garden so, in my mind, it would be plain sailing.

The evening before the ride I loaded up Stan fully for the first time. Obviously I know now that this wasn't entirely Ideal preparation for a 300 plus mile jaunt. Also, the most miles that I had managed in a day ride to date was thirty seven with no panniers or camping gear at all, so any doubtful confidence that I may have displayed up to this point was totally misplaced. To that end, I had a very wobbly few hundred metres around the locality, up one Avenue and back down another, finally declaring all to be well with the load. I disrobed Stan of his cargo (I'm sure that I heard him let out a sigh) and double checked all of my gear prior to a fairly sleepless night.

3   Those Pesky Frenchies!

We were all up and ready early in the morn. Gail and Jodie had decided that after abandoning me at my planned start point just over the Welsh border near Chepstow, that they would indulge in a girly shopping trip to Cribbs Causeway near Bristol before driving back home.

With Stan secured to the bike carrier, which was (hopefully) secured to the car, and all of my gear packed in the back we set off for Wales around 8am with me driving in my padded cycling shorts under my normal shorts. In high spirits we made it the three miles to the M20 and then.............we came to a stop. It seemed that the entire South East road network was at a virtual standstill, completely blocked with lorries of varying sizes, mainly gigantic juggernauts that were stuck in an event that we, in this region, seemed to celebrate each time either the French fishermen blocked their ports or striking militant French dock workers or whatever blocked their ports or rampaging and sometimes violent illegal immigrants blocked their ports. This time it appeared that all of these groups were conspiring to bring the county of Kent to a grinding halt. This particular time it had already been going on for a couple of weeks, causing gridlock. The Authorities decided, in their wisdom, that it would be a brilliant Idea to park all of these trucks on a section of the M20 from Maidstone almost to the coastal Port, a distance of some thirty odd miles, blocking the entire coast bound side of the motorway. This, they named *"Operation Stack"*. Us local folk had many other names for it though.

It strangled the life out of the area every time some Frenchmen got the hump. What annoyed a lot of people was the fact that there was, and still is, a large disused airport at Manston near Dover that would have taken most of the trucks off the motorway, plus other areas that would have kept local traffic moving, but it didn't seem to bother the powers that be that they were disrupting everybody's lives in South East Kent with a problem that had nowt to do with us. What's more, it was completely buggering up my day!

It took two hours to travel ten miles to Ashford. There, as we were finally diverted from the motorway, I had a cunning plan. I would drive north towards Faversham (totally the wrong way to the way that I wanted, but that wouldn't be the only time before this quest was completed).

We reached the slip road for the M2 when I decided that I needed to release some liquid. I parked up in a type of lay by (I think that it was a hard shoulder really), climbed the barrier, went into the bushes...... and trod straight into a pile of what appeared to be dog's doodah. Oh terrific! After attending to my task and then wiping clean my trainer in the long grass I returned to the car to be greeted by sniffs and screwed up noses from my female staff.

The journey continued with several further delays on the M25. It dawned on us that I would never be able to cycle the fifty odd miles from Wales to Holt as it was already early afternoon so it was agreed that I would start somewhere off the M4 between Bristol and Bath to have any chance of reaching the day's destination. A compromise was being made already.

We left the motorway at junction 18 and found a country lane between Yate and the village of Todmarton. I offloaded Stan and packed him up like a donkey ready for a trek over the Alps (I'm not sure if any laden donkey has actually made that journey, but if it had, that's what he would have looked like). I did a couple of hundred yard runs up and down the road to get accustomed to the feeling of pedalling the weighty monster, a few photos were taken of the not so intrepid traveller and then it was time to depart.

When we left home I had what felt like a stomach full of moths, now they had turned into fully grown butterflies. A big hug and a concerned look from Gail and a quick hug and a sarcastic comment from Jodes and I was on my way. I was really cheesed off that I wouldn't be crossing the Severn Bridge on the trip but, due to the nice Frenchies, it really wasn't a viable option. The main thing was that I was on my way, my girls were going to look around the shops prior to their long drive home and all of my plans and dreams for this had finally (almost) come to fruition. My ride wasn't to be as long as I was starting possibly thirty miles nearer but I should have clocked up at least two hundred and seventy miles plus by the end.

As the girls disappeared from view I realized I was on my own. All of the talk and the boring of everyone with my plans had ended, now it was time to get my pedals turning for a brilliant adventure. Well that was my thought as I trundled along a country road towards the village of Marshfield, near Bath.

I freewheeled down a slight hill and as I started to pedal up the incline out of the dip in the land there was a sort of *"CRUMP"* noise from the back. The bike came to a sudden jolting stop and I shot forward, resting my Gentleman's region on the low crossbar. *"WHAT THE ####"* I may have retorted as I just about regained my balance and let Stan roll to a forty five degree angle. I dismounted as gingerly and as quickly as I could as I was on a bend in the road at the time. I tried to push Stan up the hill but the back wheel was firmly stuck so I had to drag him up to a side junction where there was room to put him on the stand and have a look at what had happened.

Oh dear, it wasn't good at all. The rim was bent and had a crack running along it, two spokes had snapped off, the tyre was flat with the outer wall stuck between the outside of the rim and the, now bent, brake section. I unloaded all of my panniers and threw them down onto the verge, turned the bike upside down and tried to free the wheel. It was buckled and wouldn't budge at all so, not really knowing what else I could do, I phoned Gail. I battled with the wheel for what felt like hours until they returned but it was, in fact, only forty minutes or so.

There was nowt that I could do. If the wheel wouldn't go round I couldn't drag it all the way home so there was only one logical option. Whilst Jodie decided to let the entire English speaking world know of my abject failure via social media, Youfacepainttube, Twatter or whatever, I reattached the bike rack to the car and loaded everything once again. I wasn't sure if the look on Gail's face was one of concern, pity or relief. A bit of each, I think. At least at the time Jodes could see the funny side although she did lecture me not to sit in the car all the way home feeling sorry for myself. She even reminded me that she had taken a day off work for me and she hadn't seen any shops, just parked trucks and motorways!

So that was it. My three hundred mile cycle tour hadn't even lasted ten miles and I was (despite Jodie's instructions) sitting in the back of the car sulking and feeling sorry for myself. If I had a tail, I would have been heading home with it firmly between my legs. Jodie had telephoned the pub at Holt and explained what had happened and I think that they must have felt so sorry for me (them as well), that they totally refunded my booking. I think that they may have chuckled a bit as well.

So I headed home, a very depressed bunny. Surely that wasn't it? It couldn't be. It had taken a year for me to pedal no more than ten miles and now I was going home with a broken bike but (I hoped) not a broken spirit. I think that it may have come as a shock to my transport crew when I said that I was going to have another go next year when I'd got over this debacle. I think that they were suitably impressed although I heard Gail sigh loudly and Jodie told me not to involve her again.

If only she had a Crystal Ball!!!!

Back at home after a long journey, thinking of what might have been, Stan and all of my gear were unloaded and after a while we all trudged off to bed. But was I actually a failure? Could I have done things differently? Were there actually any flaws in my plans? Or was I just struck down with the curse of *"Mister Lucky"* yet again? The answer on all counts was *"Yes"*, of course it was.

4 A new Dawn

I couldn't face getting on a bike again for a couple of weeks and when I did, it was just along the canal on Eric, my mountain bike (yes, I had names for everything, especially bikes). I took Stan to Ben, my bicycle repairman to get him fixed then I asked him to try to sell Stan as I'd lost a lot of confidence in him. Apparently the wheels, and especially the spokes were made from inferior Chinese metal and the weight of just me at eleven stone (Writer's licence there) at the time was enough to snap them, never mind the bags and camping gear.

Stan was sold to a retired Army chap for just pootling about on and selling him is something that I regret to this day. I'm a big softie at heart and I've always felt the same about my cars as well.

After Stan's departure, put out to grass for a less torturous life, Gail and myself found Nobby the Nomad at a cycle shop in Ashford. He was a Giant (not a massive bike. That was the make). He was a Hybrid Touring bike, much lighter with double thickness wheel rims and extra strong spokes (vital for my confidence). He had all of the correct gearing, including a Granny gear, and with a few adjustments to the cables, new higher handlebars, a suspension seat post and new front low rider pannier racks that I fitted on, he looked and felt the part. He was actually measured for me, or I was for him, I can't remember. Anyway, Nobby the Nomad was born.

Out I went over the ensuing months as I altered my plans and route and generally prepared for my second attempt at my massive (to some ,pathetic) challenge. I went out almost on a daily basis, doing anything from a paltry five up to thirty odd miles in a day, always with Nobby unloaded of course, apart from drinks etc. I know that even thirty miles wasn't enough for my envisaged daily mileage on the tour but if you are going to run a marathon you don't run one every day in practice, you build up to it. That was my theory anyway. If I could cycle fifty miles in a day now, where was the challenge in doing it for real on the trip? Flawed logic, possibly? Anyway the most that I managed that summer was forty seven. Once!

I still couldn't get anyone to do the ride with me although, to be honest, even though I was still a bit scared by it all I was actually looking forward to doing it by myself. As long as I was sensible with everything, drinking, eating, realistic mileage etc. I would or should be fine.

What did I know?

This time my plan was to drive myself to my friend's house in Gloucester, cycle to the train station, catch a train to Chepstow and cycle home from the Welsh border via the Severn bridge (this time, please!). I booked only my first B&B (again) at a lovely farmhouse in Semington along the Kennett & Avon canal. The rest would just fall into place. I wasn't nicknamed *Jonah Lucky* for nowt ! But now was the time to put that myth to bed.

5   A Bridge not too far

Nobby, all ready to go. Note the much needed camping gear!

My July departure date arrived once more. I drove Gail to work, went home and loaded Nobby and my gear in Vera the Almera (Yep, sad I know), and on the bright Wednesday morn, off I went. Jodie and Ralph the cat had wished me luck (I think). It was a gentle easy drive up to my start point this time with only a couple of hold ups and detours to find a secluded wooded spot to empty my bladder (I don't like motorway services and public toilets, I know, I'm strange that way) and upon my arrival in the beautiful city of Gloucester I enjoyed a pleasant dinner and evening being mercilessly ribbed and ridiculed by Neil about the ride. He prefers motorbikes and jigsaw puzzles. His totally upsetting and, I must say, horrendously insulting behaviour was equalled out by his lovely wife, Andi, who fussed, fretted and generally worried about my welfare on the days ahead. They were chalkiest chalk and the cheesiest cheese. Andi didn't know it at the time but she would have a lot more anxiety before I had completed my quest.

After a restless night and a breakfast of tea, toast and ridicule (I think that Neil was secretly jealous, though he hid it very well!) it was time to go. It took a while to get all of my much needed equipment secured, and to good wishes and damp eyes from Andi and giggles and damp trousers from Neil, I cast off and wobbled and weaved my way through the rush hour traffic to the station.

If there is one place that I know quite well its Gloucester. But that's either on foot or from a car. I missed my turning and had to back track to the station. I'd already bought my ticket to Chepstow so, after being helped through the barriers, I was on the platform awaiting my train. When it arrived at 8.58am on time, I boarded and wheeled Nobby into position in the cycle section. I stood by him as he swayed about. I could sense fellow passengers looking at us, perhaps wondering where our adventure was heading, perhaps admiring us in a *"wish I were doing that"* sort of way, but more than likely, they were laughing to themselves as they viewed an overloaded pushbike accompanied by a bloke looking like a cross between Rod Stewart and a Chuckle brother with legs borrowed from a bandy legged budgie! Oh I do hope not.

Nobby on the train to Chepstow

I could see the Severn from the train window and then, as we neared Chepstow, I believe we skirted the River Wye. In my opinion, it's the prettiest river in Britain, although not this bit.

I disembarked at Chepstow station and stood on the platform as the train departed. The exit was on the other platform over the track so I heaved, humped and struggled to drag my beast of burden up and over the footbridge and then down the other side, inwardly and outwardly cursing at the lack of a ramp, a lift or any assistance when I spotted the ramp and track crossing at the other end of the platform. Oh bugger!!!!

Still, things can only improve from here, I thought. I pushed Nobby out of the station, checked my trusty highlighted map, saw that I should turn left after a few metres, mounted, said "Here *we go*" to myself and set off. At the left turn I saw a hill as steep as a wall leading off into the distant clouds so off I got and started to push and push and push. My hip, spine and legs were screaming out to me to stop, which I had to do every fifty metres or so. I was very hot as well as I very slowly climbed up through the back roads, not too sure if I was heading the correct way.

I approached a chap who was cleaning his car to ask for directions. What a nice friendly man he was. He asked me all about my trip, I showed him my map and he studied it, frowned, and informed me that I was nowhere near where I thought I was on the map. He told me that he was originally from Kent and then he insisted on walking with me for a few yards to ensure that I got onto the right road. On his departure he grasped my hands, wished me a good journey and pressed something into my palm.

It was a leaflet. He said that it was something to read on the way. It turned out that it was a Christian leaflet. Although I'm not at all religious, I still have that leaflet in my bar bag to this day. What a thoroughly nice and helpful person he was. Perhaps it was a good omen, only time would tell.

I eventually reached a main road and the writing on the road stated "*ARAF*" or "*STOP*" and there were all sorts of different signage in both Welsh and English. I stopped by a Welcome to Wales sign "*Croeso I Gymru*". I was actually in Welsh Wales.

Heading (hopefully) in a South Easterly direction I, almost by accident really, found the cycle lane beside the M48 and there, all of a sudden, was a sight that I had waited over a year to see. The Severn

Bridge! Not the newer Severn Bridge, the old original much prettier one (Also the only one that you're allowed to cycle over). As I crept towards it I must admit that I was filled with emotion (not emulsion, I'm not into guzzling water based paint). I know that people cross it on their bikes all of the time but this was a dream for me. I live on the other side of the country and never thought that I would do this. I was glad that I was wearing my sunglasses just in case the breeze had made my eyes go a bit watery. I pulled up and set up my little portable recorder in its holder on the handlebars. I wanted this bit recorded.

Crossing the Wye, then up to the Severn whilst chatting away to the recorder! Hmmm.

The first section took me over the River Wye on a raised platform, then up and onto the main span of the bridge. It was both sunny and glorious with views to the North of the Royal Forest of Dean and to the South of Wales and the newer M4 Bridge. This actual bridge was fifty years old this year, as a larger banner informed me.

"YES, I'M ACTUALLY DOING IT, I'M CROSSING THE SEVERN" I sang out to the recorder and posterity. It was a steady gentle upward pedal to the middle of the bridge where I stopped to take a couple of pictures, then it was downwards again to the English side, with me chuntering away, giving a commentary all the way. I left the bridge and passed the sign for England.

Heading to England over the Severn bridge

After a while I pulled up to check the map and turn the recorder off. BUGGER!!!!!! I hadn't turned it on. I was sure that I had but there was no red *"Record"* button on, all of that non-recording and non-commentary. My jinx had struck again. At least I had the photographs. I promised myself that I wouldn't make that mistake again.

I was looking for the village of Aust (pronounced *"ost"* I believe) so I asked a farmer who was shutting a gate after shepherding a flock of cows through (I told you I was a country boy). I showed him where I thought I was on the map and he pointed to a place at least a thumb's width away. Oh dear.

I told him that I wanted to head to tockington so he made me about turn as I had passed the required junction."*Yus bint garn wrungun,yus ned garn yunder wap"* I interpreted his directions as.

My map reading needed to drastically improve or else, at this rate, I could end up in either Carlisle or Cornwall. I stopped for a drink beside the very posh Tockington Manor school and accosted yet another local, this time a lady dog walker (You never seem to get a dog lady walker). I wanted to know that I was on the correct road. I was definitely not going to trust my inadequate map reading skills at this time. She cheerily told me (in a rather posh accent, not a yokel) that I was okay but that there was a bit of a hill coming up before I reached the A38 Gloucester to Bristol road. Apparently the A38 runs from Bodmin in Cornwall to Mansfield in Nottinghamshire and it's the longest two digit A road in England at 292 miles or 470km. Another pointless statistic that I expect you already knew. I prefer to ponder on such posers as *"Who taught the three bears how to make porridge?"*

I made my way along a lovely hedge lined country lane until the road started to steadily climb. I mouthed to myself *"keep going, keep going, keep......."* I had to get off and push. The hill, though not too steep, got steeper (Does that make sense?) and it must have taken me almost half an hour to reach the top and the junction where I collapsed onto a bench that was conveniently placed for poor souls such as myself.

There was a decision to be made, to the Left or Right? I consulted the map. Well, Right was Bristol so Right it was. I was then looking for a left turning according to my map. I stopped again and asked at a garage but, unbelievably, the chap didn't know where there was such a turning, so I did an about turn (not the first today) and pedalled the mile or so back past my recovery bench and onwards in a Northerly direction towards Gloucester.

Just when it seemed that I was doomed to cycle back to Andi and Neil's house and total ignominy, a likely looking turning appeared and without a second thought or instruction from me, Nobby headed off along it.

It was a B road, the B4427 to be precise and it was fairly busy with no path or cycle lane but that was fine. It was a hot sunny day with hardly any breeze and I was cycling in South Gloucestershire heading for (fingers crossed) the Bristol/Bath cycleway, although I didn't have a Scooby Doo where it may be. With a happy heart I crossed over the M5 motorway, if it was any other motorway I was in trouble!

At Earthcott Green I swung right, still on the same B4427, though heading towards Hambrook according to the sign. These were the type of country roads that I had pictured in my mind. "Perfick" as Pop Larkin would have said. I was even singing to myself although perhaps Nobby would have covered his ears... if he had ears.... or hands to cover them with.

I had been carrying plenty of water and some nibbly type food (squashed steak slices, flapjacks etc.) but I kept putting off stopping for a proper break, eager to get to Bath first. Apart from the earlier hills it had been really pleasant cycling with very little effort, letting the gears do most of the work. Despite the heavy load Nobby was purring along. Soon I would be crossing the M4..... There it was! Another major highway out of the way.

Now I believed that I was on the top end(ish) of Bristol or thereabouts. All of a sudden I was in a built up area and at a quite large busy junction. Again, as I couldn't work it out from the map, I asked directions from an unlucky passerby. After acknowledging his instructions and thanking him, I headed off in completely the opposite direction. Realizing my error after a few hundred metres I turned round and cycled back past him looking suitably foolish. He just looked the other way.

I did recover, and following his guide I found my route. I was actually pedalling along with the M4 beside me on my left then, veering to the right, I passed over the M32 into Bristol.

Then there was a massive intersection to be crossed. Luckily there were major road works so the traffic was moving slower than a badger with sore feet (I honestly don't know where that came from). I was helped over the carriageway by some really helpful road workers. They must have recognised a kindred spirit as road working was my career for over thirty years. Or maybe it was because they saw that I was struggling to keep Nobby upright, never mind push him across the road. I asked one of them if I was on the right road for the cycleway but he said that he came from Cardiff and he didn't have a clue. *"That's two of us"* I said.

Anyway, I eventually found myself on the edge of some parkland near a place called Downend. I looked up at some signs and there it was.....a pointer to the Bristol/Bath cycleway. It was all downhill and hairpin bends to start with. In fact it never went uphill at all on the way to Bath. I had about ten miles or so of easy riding, sharing with walkers and many other cyclists (although I didn't see any fellow cycle tourists).

Pretty soon I was pootling alongside the River Avon as it headed into Bath. Before too long I was off Nobby and weaving my way through pedestrians whilst looking for somewhere to take a break. I found a little park in Queen Square opposite the very swanky looking Francis Hotel. It was then that I felt really faint and had to hold onto a post to stop myself from stumbling and possibly passing out. What a berk! I realized that I was quite dehydrated and hungry so I sat on a bench and emptied my panniers of even more squashed steak slices, crisps, bananas and a flapjack. I would have to find somewhere to replenish my water supply as well. A tap or fountain would do if I couldn't get some in a shop. I wasn't going to pay tourist rates though. I wasn't that sort of tourist.

Nobby, chillin' in Queen Square, Bath

It was about 3pm and I must confess that I loved being there, well and truly on my trip and coping well (Okay, not well but I was coping) I called Gail and let her know how I was doing, leaving any worrying bits out. Not that there were any. After a good several minutes rest (I can't stay still for too long) I led Nobby through the city streets full of summer tourists.

I heard *"Wish you were here"* by Pink Floyd wafting over the crowds and then spotted the performer of the song. It wasn't David Gilmour. It was a brilliant street busker (put "Bath Busker" into youfacetube), I dallied a while as he was really good, then I headed off to Poultney Bridge, past Gloucester RFC's nearest rival's Bath's Recreation Ground stadium. Despite being a Gloucester boy at heart I have to admit that Bath have a really pretty ground (Ooh that hurt).

Riding around for a bit, I asked a lady where the Kennett and Avon canal might be. *"Up the hill through Sydney Gardens"* she said. I said *"A canal, up a hill ?"*, She laughed *"That's Bath for you!"*

I found Sydney Gardens and pushed Nobby up through the flowers and shrubs until I arrived at a couple of steps, up them and through a railed fence and there it was, The Kennett and Avon Canal, and I was going to cycle along it, another dream about to come true. I took a few moments to savour the occasion and snap a couple of photos.

I was feeling quite chipper again. Despite my somewhat inauspicious start earlier in the day, using my uncanny sense of direction and, it has to be said, my almost unbelievable map reading and navigational skills I had made it from Wales to this point. Okay I know that in the great scheme of things that it wasn't a major achievement. In fact for many cyclists it wasn't even an achievement at all but for this disabled ageing old hippy with broken bits comparable to an almost new Austin Allegro, two weeks off the production line, and with an apparent total lack of ability to either tell North from South or East from West, it could've been seen as a damned miracle!!!!

Without further bluster and to prove my point, I aimed Nobby to the Right, mounted and just prior to pushing off, asked an elderly gent if it was the way to Bradford on Avon. *"Naw !"* he said *"That way be Bristol"* Oh! *"I bet you be glad you arsked me now"* He laughed. Hopefully he was laughing with me and not at me. Also, I may have slightly exaggerated his accent as well!

I had to dismount to turn Nobby around as the tow path wasn't that wide. A quick dunking wouldn't have been very pleasant in the Bisto gravy coloured water. Pointing the correct way I gingerly cycled off. At least now if I kept next to the canal I might make my evening's destination of Semington.

LEFT! That's the correct way to Bradford on Avon

It was a brilliantly sunny late afternoon and the water's edge was lined with narrow boats and other boats of all shapes and sizes.

There was even one boat shaped like a sort of stealth submarine. You just had to smile at the imagination of some folk. I got many a greeting or wave as I slowly made my way along. I didn't want to rush this section, even if I could, which I couldn't as there were too many people about, walking, cycling, jogging. It was a truly blissful period of the journey.

Cycling along, it was easy to view both the railway line and the River Avon in places as they ran almost parallel to the canal. I wondered if the canal folk realized how lucky they were to live here. I'm sure they did. The scenery in the valley, for that's what it was, was incredibly stunning. To take it all in took some doing. The surrounding hills, scattered with woodland, farm stock and the occasional house were something to behold. If I was afforded only one memory of the trip it would have to be this canal. Even holidaymakers, chugging along on hire boats, smiled and waved. When I say *"chugging along"* that was in my imagination as most of the boats were electric powered. It would have perhaps been a better description to have said *"Glided along"*.

It was a journey of only about fifteen miles from Sydney Gardens to Semington but each mile was memorable. I was so chuffed to have included this bit on my trip, in fact if I'm being honest this and the Severn crossing were two of the main reasons for doing this particular route, and I was seeing both on day one. My other landmark on the canal, the Caen Flight at Devizes would come on day two, if I make it that far.

The canal wound its way between the hills as it headed to Bradford on Avon and crossed the river on the Dundas aqueduct where I switched to the opposite side of the canal. At the Avoncliff Aqueduct I steered Nobby, at first over, and then under the Aqueduct and came back out on the left side again. The path continued to the marina at Bradford on Avon where I took out a loan to buy a sad person's pot of tea for one. I parked Nobby beside me and sat at a table just taking in the scene. At the risk of continually repeating myself, I had dreamt, nay , yearned for moments like this on my journey. I was considerably more than knacked. I'd never actually cycled any distance at all with a heavily laden bike so, in all ways, this was all new ground for me. The marina was alive with people working on boats and holiday makers taking in the scenery just like myself.

The river and railway line, as seen from the aqueduct

After a restorative cuppa and some snacks I was ready to continue the last little bit to my B&B. I passed through Hilperton marina and, cycling down from a bridge onto a, now, much narrower path, one of my front panniers slipped and got caught in the wheel, almost having me over and into the canal. Luckily I tipped the other way and tumbled into some nettles and one or two very thorny brambles that made me wince and holler a bit.

I managed to lift Nobby off the path and out of people's way and re-secured the scuffed pannier to the front rack. To be honest it wasn't such a bad thing to just have a reminder to keep a check on things regarding Nobby and his baggage as I think that I'd just assumed that all would be fine without checking. I could have done without the nettles and brambles though as they hurt.

I reached the bridge leading to the village of Semington and pedalled up through the high street past the Somerset Arms public house to the roundabout where I turned left onto the A361 to Devizes. My bed for the night was about a mile along at a lovely farmhouse. On arrival, my hosts welcomed me as if they were actually very pleased to see me despite the horrible, stung, bleeding, worn out and sweaty state of me.

The man of the house, Derek, showed me into a large metal barn (no, not my room) where Nobby would spend the night locked up with a classic Austin 10 and Austin 12. They were definitely old enough to babysit him. Derek told me, with obvious pride that they attend most of the classic car shows in South West England and beyond. I must confess that I lingered for a long time looking at the cars, but I do love old vehicles, they have a character that newer motors would never have a hope of attaining. I would have an old Austin A35 or another Austin A55 tomorrow (I had one some years ago) but I think, in fact I know that Gail would disagree one hundred per cent. But what does she know? She can't drive!

Whilst in the barn, Carole, the lady of the house had made me a pot of tea with cake and biscuits which I enjoyed sitting in the evening sun in the garden. My room had its own entrance at the side of the house and from the window I could see several air balloons to the west in the setting sun. Carole had recommended that I had porridge in the morn for slow release energy instead of a fried breakfast. I readily agreed as I love porridge and it made good sense. There would be toast, homemade jams, cereals and fruit on offer too (I was being spoilt).

My room had absolutely everything that I needed, Tea, coffee and biscuits, TV and a bath to soak in.

I worked it out that I had ridden approximately 55 miles today. It was more than it should have been and far more than I'd ever done before. Also, I hadn't really eaten at all well nor had I drunk as much as I should have done. My plans on finding burger vans and roadside cafes hadn't materialized at all. There just weren't any, nor were there any little village shops that I passed en route. I realized that things would have to improve on the sustenance front and the daily mileage would possibly need to reduce as I wouldn't be able to sustain this kind of mileage with such a heavy load, especially if I couldn't replenish my food and drink supplies to turn into energy. All of these things had to improve. No engine can run for long on empty.

Of course when I telephoned Gail I told her that all was going well, as it was. I also told her what I needed to do during the next day. I told her that I was going to stick to country lanes and roads, saunter over Salisbury Plain and take on board plenty of food and drink and not push to get too far.

Have a guess what happened?

I had a lovely long soak in the bath then washed my padded cycling undershorts in the same water. You can't buy class. I then chilled out on my bed reading until I retired for the night. Day one had been completed.

6 The Banana incident!

Friday morning dawned a bit greyer but still warm. After enjoying a brilliant early breakfast consisting of all of the things I'd mentioned, I retrieved Nobby , thanked his babysitters, and loaded him up, with the extra burden of my wet and heavy cycle shorts stretched out across the back rack to hopefully dry. I asked Carole if I could take any fruit and she told me to help myself. I took a couple of bananas, more of which may be spoken about much later that day. This was my first ever time in any type of B&B guesthouse and I couldn't see that this particular farmhouse could ever be bettered. I was made so welcome and felt so comfortable there. I couldn't thank Carole and Derek enough for being a part of my journey.

I bid them both farewell and followed instructions back to the canal, out along the A361 then after a few hundred metres, left down a little lane and back beside the water and on to Devizes. It was all quiet along the towpath this early in the day. I had soon passed the Devizes camping and caravanning site and the Foxhangers campsite by Caen Hill marina. These sites I had marked down on my map as possible emergency campsites. It seems ridiculous now as they were only a couple of miles or so down from my B&B.

 At last I stopped by the Caen Hill bottom lock. This time I got my mini recorder out and made sure that the red record button was on. I wasn't going to get caught out again. I may not be bright, I may not be intelligent, but at least I'm stupid……. Hang on, I think I'm missing a "*not*" out there!

Anyway, with a good thrust forward on the left pedal I started the steady slow climb up to the top. I got several shouts of encouragement and general good natured banter from folk on board their craft in the various sections of the flight. I plodded up, determined not to have to get off and push. Not here.

I rode Nobby past the 29 locks that rise by 237 feet in two miles. A gradient of 1 in 44, allegedly. Actually I Googled that fact when I got home, if I'd guessed I might have said *"A rise of approximately 1237 feet"* as that's what it felt like. Once I had reached level ground at the top I stopped, made sure that the red button was still recording (it was), switched it off then carried on into Devizes town.

At the bottom of the Caen flight

I headed for the town centre. Stopping at a garage to top up with drinks and snacks, I saw a sign for Upavon along the A342. This wasn't an ideal road but I thought that I would use it until I could get onto little winding lanes. Hmmmm.

The morning sky was clouding over, the road wasn't a wide one but seemed like quite a fast one, if the way that I was being buffeted about was anything to go by.

A chocolate zoomed past me doing 100mph, hmmm, I thought, that must be a *"Ferrari Rocher!"*

The path on the opposite side, when it was there, was very narrow and overgrown so I opted to stay where I was.

The rolling Wiltshire hills and countryside spread out before me. There was a fair old headwind at times in the open country but I pressed on. Upavon would only be a few miles down the road. I could regroup there, check my map, find my marked out route and continue on that. It couldn't be that hard!

Most of the traffic gave me a decent amount of space and I always raised my hand and smiled to thank them but there were one or two hairy moments, especially with large trucks that didn't appreciate losing all of their speed.

Although there always appeared to be hills in front of me in the distance the road chose to either skirt around them or cut through with hardly any discernable rise or fall. This, I was immensely grateful for. I passed through the village of Cherton at a steady 12mph which wasn't too bad against a stiff breeze. A bit of sun would have been welcome but at least it was dry and I could see all around for miles.

By this time it was just solid road and verges with no option other than to keep going. By heck, this area was open to the elements and I assumed it to be the top end of Salisbury Plain. A right turn and just down the road was the turn off for Upavon.

I had a break on a grass verge at the junction. There was a convenient bench and litter bin there so I took advantage of both. On parking Nobby on his stand I noticed that the front rack holding the right side pannier had come loose. I had lost the bolt that fixed it to the front fork and the rack was just hanging on that side. No need for panic though as I carried a supply of cable ties so I just threaded one through the holes to secure it. I thought that it would suffice until I reached a bike shop. Quite pleased with my little victory over slight adversity, I sat down and ate an oaty bar and banana and had a drink. I thought that I'd save the other piece of succulent fruit until later.

I noted that the A345 would take me to Amesbury, so replacing my map case on my handlebars, off I went. Even I shouldn't get lost on a main road. I did feel that I was cheating from my Ideal a bit but I had become obsessed with selecting a goal or town and reaching it the easiest, quickest way. I was starting to lose a bit of focus regarding the tour. I was sure that I would recover it at Amesbury though, after I'd found some lunch as the litterbin that I'd just left didn't have any food in it, only a wrapper and my old banana skin.

The A345 carried on in the same vein as the A342, but with a few more trees to protect me from any wind in places. I really knew that I was crossing the Plain as there were tank signs and crossing places along the road although, to my disappointment, I didn't actually see any tanks.

It was a bit more undulating here but I had the momentum to keep in the saddle. My little sparrow legs were obviously firming up and the whirring motion of the wheels allowed my mind to wander, not about the mundane things that I'd planned. Like naming my top ten Dire Straits, Pink Floyd and David Bowie tracks, nor trying to remember the first 75 Subbuteo team colours from my childhood (Something that I can sometimes actually do!)

No, more to Tim Vine like stuff such as *"If ghosts can walk through walls, why don't they fall through floors?"* or *"Who did the first person to catch a cold catch it off?"* Yep, it's a strange old world being a cyclist with too much time to think. Here's one to finish on for now, *"If money doesn't grow on trees, then why do banks have branches?"* Answers on a postcard!

Anyway, too much digression there, so back to the road which I'd been on for nearly four hours now today. I was starting to feel a bit jaded and I think that I needed to get off the main A roads as soon as possible after a stop in Amesbury.

Durrington was reached and after a short pause on a bench by the roundabout (I seemed to like benches) I continued on into Amesbury via a major roundabout with the famed A303. This was a *"Pedal like the clappers"* type of junction as everybody in their metal boxes of various sizes seemed to be in a hurry. It was a heads down, clear signal, and go for it moment. I survived, just.

My little stroke of good fortune. The cycle shop on the Left and my little picnic bench, ahead on the Right.

Amesbury certainly gave off an air of affluence as I made my way into the town centre. I couldn't believe my luck as at the first mini roundabout was Hills cycle & Fishing Tackle shop. Well, I don't do fishing. I would rather spoon feed cornflakes to an irritated Hippo than sit on a riverbank or seashore for hours just looking at the water (each to their own, I suppose) but I did need my front rack repair checking out so in I went. The very nice shop owner informed me that my handiwork would easily see me home so no need for any replacement bolt. That was good news indeed. I was a pukka bike mechanic now.

I headed off down the main street and, ignoring Aldi, found a bakery where I agreed to donate some internal organs plus a lot of money for a pasty and a sausage roll. I never seemed to learn. I took my, not so cheap, but hot pastries back to a bench (another one) by a car park at the junction and had my lunch. Jodie then called me and on hearing where I was, told me that I had just passed within a couple of miles of Stonehenge. I wasn't even aware, that's how blinkered I had become. Also I had passed by Woodhenge, which, until then, I had never even heard of. Hey Ho!

As I sat there it started to rain, it had been threatening to for a while. I don't mean that it had been shouting at me or anything. It was just that the clouds had been getting darker.

I made sure that my panniers and gear were as waterproof as they could have been. A bright yellow purpose built waterproof cover for the back bags and mainly bin liners for the front, and I put on my waterproof hooded jacket. This managed to keep my top half dry anyway.

So off I pedalled in the rain, out of Amesbury until I started to climb up a hill. My legs just couldn't propel me up it and so I had to get off

Nobby and push. It was two lanes on my side with no chance of getting out of the traffic. I just stayed as close to the edge as I could and shuffled along very slowly. My right hip and spine were really protesting at this point and I honestly thought that I may have needed medical assistance for the first time, but instead I chose to shout at myself *"You chose to do this, now just get on with it"* and other encouraging chants and curses.

A sort of slip road lay by appeared and I needed no second bidding to get off the main drag for a bit. There was a sign that stated *"NO DUMPING"* but I was okay as I only wanted a wee!

I did rejoin the main road further on after a breather and it had by now levelled out. I just kept pedalling now. All I knew was that at some point I needed to get off this road to Salisbury and head across country to Porton, and in the general direction of Winchester. I didn't really have much of a clue what I was doing or where I was going. Nothing new there!

It was wet, really wet now and this was definitely not a pleasant road to be on at all. I saw a sign for Porton and at last I was finally able to get off the main road. The new road took me along the side of a high chain linked fence with barbed wire on top. It was Boscombe Down Airfield according to my map. Mind you, my map was many many years old. Certainly in the rain and murk it didn't look a very welcoming place.

I spotted some trees ahead and as I needed what Americans call a "comfort break" I pulled over. I hadn't managed one back down the road as there were too many people about, sitting in their cars and vans staring out of misted up windows at the blue clad loony pushing a soaking wet bike. There certainly wasn't much comfort adding to the dampness of the area.

My shorts were soaked, by rain I mean, and my trainers were wet so there was nowt else to do but to plod on. In the bleakness of this early afternoon even the cars had their lights on so I thought that I should do the same. Only they were buried deep in my panniers that were all covered up so I had to go without. Not good planning at all. I would have to remember for next time. At least I didn't say that I would *"Learn lessons"* like so many folk seem to say on TV these days when they've goofed completely and others have lost out or suffered as a result. Ooh that winds me up!

I crossed the A338 into Porton and stopped at a local general store to stock up again on drinks, Mars bars and other sweeties and sandwiches for later. I hadn't really thought about where I was going to stay yet. I was favouring the Idea of a B&B over a campsite due to the dampness and my tiredness but I hadn't started to make any plans so far. I felt that I would cover many more miles yet.

The road continued on. There were signs saying "No Parking" "No Photographs" "No Stopping" & "No Peeping". I may have made one of those up but that was the feeling that came from behind the high fence.

It was only when I got home that I found out that it was actually Porton Down M.O.D. Defence Science & Technology Laboratory. Blimey, that's a mouthful, one of the United Kingdom's most secretive Military Research Facilities, scary or what? There certainly felt that there was an air of menace there. Perhaps that's the wrong word but I must confess to turning the pedals a bit quicker in that area.

After I cleared my own *"Twylight Zone"* I met the junction of the A30 and turned left or Eastward. This narrow fast main road was not a place for a tired old long haired geek on a heavily laden pushbike to be so I turned the wheels as if the Devil himself was after me and even then it felt like I had created a tailback stretching back to Devon.

At last I reached Lopcombe Corner and I branched off, still on the A30 though, to Stockbridge. The sky had started to brighten a bit and the rain had finally stopped by now and I mooched along trying to either sing or whistle to myself and to keep positive thoughts in my head. Do you know that there are twice as many eyebrows in the world than people?

The road itself was reasonably straight and with gentle peaks and troughs and despite being enclosed by verges and hedgerows the traffic wasn't so bad. I crossed the River Test after descending a short hill. I got the feeling that I'd have to climb again to leave Stockbridge. I would get very short odds on it. I don't gamble though, I would have £5 on the Dalai Lama if I was a Tibetan man! (It gave me a chuckle, anyway)

I was through the town before I knew it and headed out on the A3057 struggling up the dreaded hill that I had rightly predicted and forced to get off and push yet again. My legs really had had enough today but still I had to carry on. I was heading towards Kings Somborne. Why? I don't really know. I just spotted the turn and went for it.

A view up the hill and out of Stockbridge

There were some uphill bits along this road, but with a few stops to help, I managed to keep moving. It wasn't my best time of the day but I thought of the feeling that I could have at the end of it, to know that I'd survived and got through it. It wasn't that bad in the great scheme of things. Last year I didn't make it ten miles.

At Kings Somborne I stopped and asked a lady for the way to Winchester. I actually showed her my map and asked if I was going the right way, pointing to my chosen route. *"Oh yes"* she said *"But you'll have to go over Farley Mount, it's a bit of a climb"*, Oh Dragonfly's" I believe I uttered. With a hearty *"Thank you"* to the smiling lady of foretold pain, I may have had a little inward weep. I turned along the back roads towards, hopefully, Winchester and its surrounding environs.

At a road junction, as it was now getting on for 5pm I called Gail to discuss my strategy for obtaining a bed for night (I was just phoning really to let her know I was still alive and what I was doing). There was only one option available to me. I had places marked on my treasured, reliable maps and sheets of paper with addresses and phone numbers marked down (as before, but not needed then). This being a Friday evening I hoped that I hadn't left it too late. I tried a couple but got no answer then at the third attempt a lady answered and told me that *"Yes, they had a single room vacancy for £35"* Result!

I told her where I was (roughly), and how long it would take me (even more roughly) to reach her B&B in Shawford to the south of the city. I let Gail know the good news then I set off from base camp at the foot of Farley Mount.

It was a steady rise at first and then it started to climb past some very pretty country houses and an old chapel, which I had to push

Nobby on past. Not because he was eager to go inside to offer up some prayers of his own for the journey, but because my little spindle like bones wouldn't turn the pedals.

The climb wasn't actually as bad or as long as I had anticipated and then, all of a sudden I was cycling along a beautiful lane in glorious evening sunshine. I even tried to convince myself that if the situation demanded it, I could wild camp in one of the adjacent fields and nobody would either mind, nor even notice. Yeah right, of course I could!

They didn't call me *"Bushtucker Man"* after my Australian Hero Mr. Les Hiddins for nothing (Look him up). Actually nobody called me that except myself.

Actually I hardly saw another person along this lane on this fine evening. That was because it was more than likely that they were all ensconced safely in their homes enjoying a nice dinner and relaxing evening whereas I, on the other hand, was pedalling away, now quite happy although also, quite flaked out. I was doing what I had wanted to do and had planned and dreamed of doing for ages. I think that I was a bit more contented because I had my destination for the night established.

I went back to singing and daydreaming again *"Why is the word LISP spelt with an S in it?"* and *" Why is the word ABBREVIATION such a long word?",* I was better off singing.

Passing Farley Mount Country Park I spotted a few parked cars and saw some people exercising dogs (perhaps it was the local *"Dogging Area"*, No, stop it!).

Then I was once again out in the true countryside, surrounded by fields and sheltered and shaded by trees. When a junction approached I guessed which was the correct way and then came to my first major intersection, as such, the A3090. I branched Right. The traffic was very light so I ignored the path and felt quite safe cruising along the byway to Hursley. It was surprisingly flat and after what I had endured, it was very welcome.

Through the village then a left turn towards Shawford, I hoped. It seemed as if the road was never ending. I had promised Gail and Jodie that I would let them know when I arrived at the B&B but that felt like many hours ago. It was now gone 7pm and I had been on the road since around 8am, and I can't emphasize enough what an enormously heavy (self inflicted, I know) load I was pulling. All I wanted to do was have a long shower and crash out on a bed but still the road continued, and then, at last, a roundabout. I tried to check my map as there weren't any relevant signs but I gave that up and just relied on my inbuilt navigational skills and blind judgement. Then there was a sign "Welcome to Compton & Shawford". Who said that I had no sense of direction, or indeed, no sense?

Now I just had to find the B&B, I was given directions by the lady that mentioned a Garden Centre but other than that, I couldn't recall, until I recognized the name of the road that I'd been given. A quick scurry along the road and I had had arrived. Thank St. Christopher for that!

I had cycled about seventy miles, some of which weren't entirely necessary and some on foot leaning heavily on Nobby and shuffling forwards in excruciating pain with a most profound limp. My hip and spine area could now really do with some respite (Did I mention I had a problem? I don't complain).

I was greeted by the lady of the house, parked Nobby in the garage (or rather the husband did) No babysitters for him tonight. I carried my panniers, following my host up to my room which was at the far end of a very nice, exceedingly large house.

My bedroom was very good with an en suite. Coffee and tea making facilities, TV and white bedding, and I mean "WHITE!!!!!!!", pillows, sheets, quilt cover, the works. I thought to myself that I mustn't make a mess here.

As the lady left, I went to lock my door. No lock. *"Excuse me"* I called out *"My door hasn't got a lock"*. *" No, we're all very friendly here"* she laughed back to me.

 All sorts of images and scenarios were whizzing through my very tired mind so I placed a chair across the door, unpacked some clean clothes, phoned Gail in case she didn't see or hear from me again, and went for a long and well deserved shower.

"By Korky the cat" (see the Dandy comic for that one), that was one brilliant powerful shower. I felt totally refreshed after it, although quite weary. I just lay on the bed and had a read of my book for a while. I made a cuppa and ate a few little snacky bits that had survived the day's adventure. In one carrier bag I found my last banana left over from the morning at Semington. It was a bit squashed so I kept it on the bag beside me on the bed whilst I munched a flapjack.

I could, through my bedroom window, see planes losing height as they prepared to land at Eastleigh Airport to the South. Planes tonight, after the balloons of last night.

As I turned to grab my tea, I noticed brownish small stain on the pure white quilt cover. OH NO!!!!!

The squashy banana had squidged through the bag and had left its mark on the linen.

Panic now set in.

I tried to get rid of the mess with some loo roll then I had a brainwave. Running the tap in the bathroom I damped my travel sponge (a baby sponge that I use when travelling) and attempted to remove the stain by scrubbing it out.

All that I achieved was to spread the smear over a much larger area and make the quilt damp! I was left with a wet patch and a banana skid mark!

What could I do?

After running round and round in ever decreasing circles (one of my favourite old sit com's), pulling my hair out (not advised at my age) and doing a Navaho war dance while sobbing, I calmed myself down a bit.

I quietly phoned Gail and Jodie and I'm sure that I could hear their laughter without the aid of a telephone. So much for concern, sympathy and advice.

It was decided that I couldn't do anything at the time so I should sleep on it (so to speak) and think of something in the morning.

Once I had got the Hyena's off the phone I calmed down to read and doze, occasionally peeping over to offending brown stain. It was still there and hadn't moved.

Note the "offending" leaky banana bag on the bed

It was starting to get dark outside now and I could clearly see the plane's lights as they passed. I had never flown but we had got our passports a couple of years ago and I had promised that we would have a holiday abroad soon. I was quite looking forward to going up in an aeroplane. It didn't hold any fears for me. I had just never had the opportunity.

Then all of a sudden there was the sound of loud heavy rock music (or noise) coming from some property over the back. It was like nothing I could recognize and it sounded absolutely terrible.

And loud!

Boy, was it loud!

It appeared that there was a party going on.

Unbelievable!

That was just what I needed right now. It was just impossible to get to sleep with that noise. It seemed as if they were playing the same tune (badly) over and over again. Give me "*Echoes*" by Pink Floyd any day. This tuneless dirge even made my guitar playing sound reasonable. I couldn't put "good" there as my family would only correct me.

I had two choices. Three if you included mass murder, which I didn't.

It was a hot summer's night, I could either close the windows completely but still hear it clearly and sweat profusely, or I could leave the windows a bit open and sweat not quite as much and hear it even more. Any which way it didn't matter as even Herbie the hard of hearing hibernating hedgehog wouldn't have been able to sleep through that row.

At least THEY were enjoying the party, if the occasional raucous laughter and cheering was anything to go by.

I watched the clock through those next few hours. I tried to relax, I tried to read, I tried to doze, even the planes had knocked it off for the night but the head bangers kept on going.

It did eventually stop just before three thirty in the morning and it took me a bit longer to actually finally doze off. It's always harder to get off to sleep when you know that you need to as you've got an early start.

Breakfast by 7.30am and off by 8am. That was my aim. I was told that breakfast didn't start until 8am on a Saturday but they would make mine early as I wanted an early start to the day. I would have been better off spending the day in bed there but I remembered the brown bit and the fact that I didn't have a door lock.

7   The Longest Day

After a good solid three hours sleep, I rose and showered and sorted and packed all of my gear ready to get away rather spritely as I had checked the quilt cover and it did look as if I had run out of toilet paper so had opted for something else to use.

I crumpled the quilt up so that it wouldn't show as I didn't have the guts to own up for my little mishap. Surely, after I'd left, they would realize that it was only banana if they sniffed it!!!!!!!!

Anyway, down to a breakfast of scrambled eggs and toast with a pot of tea and orange juice. It was very good. I took out the money to pay and was told that it was £40. *"I thought it said £35?"* I questioned. *"No, £40"* she replied. I knew that it had stated £35 but, after banana soiling the bed linen, I thought that it was best not to argue. I asked instead about the noise last night and was informed that *"Yes it was a party, yes the music was very loud and diabolical and that some of the other guests here had gone to it and had come back in very late"*.

"No discount for my disturbed night?" I almost said out loud, but didn't have the bottle to.

I got my panniers, checked that I'd not left owt (apart from you know what), crumpled the quilt a bit more (I thought that it might help) and hurried down to load Nobby, who had conveniently been brought to the front of the house. I said my thanks and goodbyes and was away down the road before the bed was stripped. Surely somebody would catch the aroma of mashed, moulded fruit before jumping to a completely undeserved wrong conclusion!

I was fully house trained (almost).

I thought I had studied the map during the evening. I had a good Idea of my route to Chichester via Waterlooville. My first major town, relatively speaking, was to be Bishop's Waltham but, in my rush to put distance between me and the skid mark I missed the turning. I was informed of this when I asked a van driver parked in a lay by. It appeared that I was almost in Eastleigh so I had to about turn once more and go back to where I should have turned.

That was a good start, indeed.

I reckon that if I was a pathfinder for Bomber Command during the Second World War then we could have found ourselves at war with Sweden or Scotland, as my navigational expertise may have needed brushing up on. Back about three miles I found the right turning and headed off hopefully in the correct direction. I crossed the River Itchen in the warm early morning sunshine. I must admit to still feeling very tired from yesterday's exertions and last night's party keeping me awake and, with that, wound up!

I passed through Colden Common on a fairly flat road. No climbing yet. There was a sign that said *"Nob's Crook"*, but he wasn't, he was purring away like a cat that had just nicked the fish off the plate and not got caught.

Ah ha! A sign and turning onto the B2177 to Bishop's Waltham. Only one map reading error so far today. Mind you, it wasn't 9am yet. It was going to be a very hot day today that much I could figure so I would need to pace myself and take on refreshments at regular intervals. Yeah right, my past track record on that count wasn't good.

The turn off for Marwell Zoo was passed. So far things were going well. It's very hard to get over to the reader the exact feeling of making such a journey, any journey, come to that. You've probably noticed how difficult it is for me to describe by you attempting to make any sense out of my poor wittering. A real wordsmith would be able to eloquently give a beautiful graphic description of the countryside along with their poetic vocabulary, using words far too long to be acceptable on "Countdown". Me? Well I'm just trying to tell it as it was, warts an' all, and how it made me feel, both at the time doing it, and now. It's so difficult to give the reader the same experience that I had. You can only really experience it by actually doing it yourself (the same as anything, I suppose).

 All I can say is that the feeling of cycling in a totally strange place, not knowing what is around the next bend or over the next hill is absolutely brilliant, even if I haven't conveyed that opinion all of the time due to fatigue. And from a bike you see and take in so much more than you could ever experience by driving.

You also come across some weird place names. On this perfect morning I cycled through Lower Upham! Yep, you couldn't make these names up. Onwards to Bishop's Waltham I went. This B2177 was one cool dude of a road. On reaching the aforesaid mentioned town the first thing that I did was stop at a Londis store on the main route in to restock supplies. Perhaps not bananas though.

Ooh, it was hot this morn. Well it was hot for lugging a heavy bike along the road. I gorged on a cold orange lolly in the shade beside the shop before continuing onwards into the town proper. I pedalled and pushed around the town until, by chance, I approached a Gent minding his own business, just about to enter his gate. I asked him for the directions to Waterlooville as that was my intended and, absolutely not, well researched route.

"Blimey, no you don't want to go that way" he said with strong conviction. *"There be Dragons!"*

Okay, he didn't say that last bit, but he did tell me that it was quite hilly, not very nice and hard to navigate through (He was obviously unaware of my uncanny skills in that department). He said that my best option was to stick to the B2177 as it was a much nicer open road, fairly flat with just one gentle climb up to a viewing area at a place called Ports Down, and it wasn't difficult at all. Remember that bit, if you would be so kind.

We had a chat over his garden gate for a while on cycling in general as he'd done a fair bit of it himself. If nothing else on this ride, I had met some really helpful, nice, friendly, genuine folk and I was so grateful for their friendliness, encouragement and advice along the way.

So, off I went on the same road (when I found it again) towards Waltham Chase and Wickham. I was ambling along at between 10/14 mph, not hammering along but not really dawdling either. The Saturday traffic was behaving itself and so was Nobby. After yesterday and last night's disruption, I was determined to pace myself and try to enjoy the experience despite my overall fatigue. And at that time, along that road, I was fairly happy with my lot.

It was summertime, and the pedalling was easy, as the song almost said, and I was looking forward to reaching this alleged viewpoint with possibly my first glimpse of the English Channel.

A little bit of faffing about at Wickham when I lost my way, but I was soon back on course (I think) and heading towards North Boarhunt and Southwick. There were a few small wooded areas or copses to keep the nearing noon sunlight at bay on this section although I couldn't, as yet, find a nice secluded place to pull off the road and be able to ease my bladder.

Ah ha! And then I came to a crossroads where a small, out of sight of the road, wooded glade gave me sufficient shelter and privacy to fertilize the undergrowth.(and to think on the Tour De France they just pull up at the side of the road, whip it out, go, push it back in and pedal off, so uncouth).

I suffered only minor nettle stings and bramble abrasions but emerged with a contented smile and a deflated bladder.

With vast abounds and a hearty sigh I partially re-fuelled and carried on along this delightful road, whilst hoping there would be no sting in its tail. If I could have seen into the future I may have caught a bus, but I blissfully toddled off happily singing and whistling to myself. Nobby didn't join in and I was grateful for that for any unfamiliar sounds, squeaks or whistles from him would have only meant problems.

I hadn't even given tonight's bed a thought at this stage as I felt that there were many more miles to pass under Nobby's wheels before the situation would need addressing.

Oh, yet again, to have had a Crystal Ball!

According to the road signs I was now only six miles from Portsmouth.

Hang on, there was a cycle lane now and the road was starting to ascend, gently at first but I could see a fair way into the distance and it was still going up.

What the ####!

My poor legs that were already tired from yesterday's hike were starting to really protest now and I knew that my muscles (for what they were) didn't have much more to give. As the climb steadily continued, with me wobbling and weaving at no more than a brisk walking pace with all of the "Lids & Lycra" weekend cyclists easily trundling past, my legs could give no more and I came to an ungainly halt.

The sun was high in the sky, its rays beating down on my sweat dripped bonce, I had no alternative but to lean on my trusty old mate and stagger onwards and upwards using mainly just my left leg for forward propulsion and trying to keep the weight and pressure off my searingly painful right hip area.

Still, I don't complain!

I draped my tea towel that I always carry on my handlebars over my head and, looking like the love child of an Arab sheikh and Waynetta Slob from the Harry Enfield show, I proceeded, head down most of the time so that the passing motorists couldn't see how red, sweat stained and pained my face was. When I did look up to see how many days away the summit was or to acknowledge cheery encouragement from a passing cyclist (or walker!) I made sure that I had a smiley unconcerned outward façade whilst inside I was burning. I mean "BURNING".

This was so obviously the "Gentle climb" that the nice chap at Bishop's Waltham was referring to. In a car it was gentle. Pushing a fourteen stone pushbike (artistic exaggeration there) it was purgatory.

As I shuffled higher, base camp disappeared at least two miles behind and below me. I couldn't believe this. The cycle/stagger lane ran out on my side and I had to cross over onto the path on the other side by the Ports Down Technology Park. It looked like some major military place with a large white building with a golf ball on top. That was one helluva teeing area! The road though, disappeared further up for about another mile. I managed to climb back on Nobby and used my Granny gear to very slowly crest the top. Good old Granny.

There was a roundabout at the top and then..."BLIMEY O'REILLY, WHAT A VIEW"

You could see for miles around. Over to Southampton, out to towards the Isle of Wight, right across the Solent and to Gosport and Portsmouth and the Paphos District of the Island of Cyprus!

Okay, perhaps not that last bit but you could see a jolly long way, especially in this sunlight. I turned towards Havant (which I think I could also see bits of) past the Fort Widley Equestrian Centre, and I pulled off at a parking area and viewpoint (Had I mentioned the views?) with a burger van that appeared to be very popular, if the amount of people eating were owt to go by.

Nobby resting at the viewpoint (I didn't get him a burger)

Part of the view from Ports Down

I thought "This'll do for me! I parked Nobby alongside some bikers and their Harley's. I thought that they would like that, and at least I knew that they would watch him while I joined the queue.

I indulged in two cheeseburgers with onions and an ice cold can of Coca Cola (other brands are available, but I chose Coca Cola) and, to this day, I still say that they are the best two burgers that I've ever eaten (either they were very, very good or I'm easy to please). Don't just take my word for it though, if you are ever near there then give it a try. Apparently they're almost a permanent fixture. I mooched around there for a while, admiring the incredible vista. This was a high point in more ways than one.

Now for a long descent and it would be downhill from now in more ways than one again, but I didn't know it at the time. I was still enjoying the euphoria of making it so far.

The downhill to Havant

This was quite a busy road now. Still the B2177 and at least I didn't have to pedal for a while but I still had to keep my tired sweaty wits about me as everyone now seemed to be in a hurry and I was just in their way. Didn't they know that I'd just climbed a mountain? I couldn't lose concentration on the road, I had to stay focussed....Now, what was I saying?

I reached Bedhampton in the borough of Havant. Now I had to work out a couple of things before I reached Havant town centre. Which would be the easiest best way onwards to Chichester? And "*Is the Hokey Cokey really what it's all about*?"

Aggh!

"*No... Idiot, just concentrate on the first thing*"

It was time to get onto the path as my mind wasn't working properly. I crossed over the M something or other, possibly the M27. It has to be said that cycling through Havant was very stressful. I turned one way then another then back again. At one point I almost found my way onto the slip road to the A27 dual carriageway, and then I even carried and pushed Nobby up a walkway and over a footbridge over the A27, only to get completely flummoxed and do the entire thing again in reverse.

After what seemed like an eternity I found and followed a road along by the train station and gradually fought my way clear of the town, hopefully in an Easterly direction. It was still only early afternoon and I'd already covered a great distance but I'd now got it into my head to try to reach the Brighton area by night time.

Another (In hindsight) mistake, only this time it would prove to be a big one.

Following the A259, the road that goes almost past my house in many more miles, I passed Southbourne and Nutbourne by using cycle lanes or footpaths where I could as it was reasonably busy on the road.

Did you know that 30% of car accidents in Sweden involve a Moose? I say *"Don't let them drive"*. Just a thought!

I reached Chichester where I had to negotiate my way either through, or around, to find the way to Bognor Regis. The good Council's of the area had at least thought of the poor cyclist as there were plenty of cycle lanes or paths alongside the road. I was very grateful to have part of my own space on the highway. It did make you feel a bit safer, especially if you were one of those folk that, for whatever reason, didn't feel happy or comfortable with a lid on their barnet.

I know, I know, some think that I'm an idiot not to wear one in these Health & Safety conscious times, but it's still a free country and a free and personal choice. I don't preach to folk either way and I certainly don't appreciate being told what I should or shouldn't do.

I feel the same about being told what I supposedly can or can't say as somebody may be offended on somebody else's behalf. I'm not talking here about extreme or obviously offensive stuff, but more about daft things like calling somebody from Ireland "Paddy" or "Jock" from Scotland. I see myself as part English (We don't seem to have a printable nick name) and part "Taffy" due to my obvious Welsh Descendancy and love of Rugby! There are far too many daft do's and don'ts around now. There was a time when we could think for ourselves and there were more important things to occupy our lives. Don't let interfering busy bodies grind us down.

There, that's another rant out of the way.

I am also aware that if I were to cycle in other certain countries I wouldn't have a choice in wearing a helmet as it's compulsory, so there. Na Na Na Na Na !

The ring road through Chichester wasn't too bad, with plenty of directional signage for Bognor. It was just a matter of being in the correct lane at times, but I was afforded a certain amount of courtesy by the many other road users.

I found myself on a dual carriageway at first heading out of Chichester with a two foot strip at the edge of the road (very unnerving), then a main road with a cycle/ footpath (Hurrah).It was only five miles to Bognor and eleven to Littlehampton (No jokes please).

Mid afternoon was creeping up and I was feeling very weary of body and mind but I kept the pedals turning. This section to Bognor was quite good on the cycle path but with not a lot to see other than fields, bushes and car dealerships.

At times the path even ventured away from the road behind bushes. That was a nice break from the traffic noise, but soon it was back. At a roundabout I saw a sign for Littlehampton (Still no jokes please) so I veered left and bypassed the town of Bognor Regis completely and somehow I rejoined the A259 further on.

With Bognor now receding behind me, I hadn't a clue where I was or where I'd been as I had just travelled on some newish roads and my up to date Ordnance Survey map for the area (Sheet 197) dated from 1983! I was more likely to find Oxon trails instead of new, up to date roads.

By the way, the word *"Receding"* is over 400 years old apparently. That's going back a bit!

There were a lot of fields on my map that aren't there now. That was yet another example of my exemplary planning. The only positive note on my map reading was my ability to mostly hold the map the correct way up, although sometimes I had difficulty doing even that. (Not really, I'm not a complete idiot. Parts of me are missing!).

Anyway, all of these roads were new to me so it didn't make no never mind really. I just had to plod on towards Brighton in the intense heat. This road now seemed never ending and with, as yet, no sign of the sea. At least I mainly still had a cycle path alongside the road. It was just as well because I was really struggling at this point.

I crossed the River Arun almost without noticing and headed through Littlehampton (Titter ye not!) on the A259 in almost a Zombie like state. It was time to take a break and to try to arrange my accommodation but typical of my weird way of overdoing things I thought that I'd get a bit further first. It was a fair while since I'd had those burgers and I wasn't recognizing the symptoms of fatigue nor dehydration.

A few miles on at East Preston I stopped in some shade by a shop. I bought an ice lolly and a nice cold drink and a Mars bar. I sat and called home and asked if Jodie could telephone my list of B&B's for the Brighton area. She wasn't a happy bunny and she couldn't believe that I'd left it so late on a mid summer's Saturday afternoon to try to get accommodation in Brighton, of all places.

Well, Jodie and Gail both tried the numerous B&B's and cheaper hotels on my list covering an area from Worthing to Peacehaven and beyond, and there were no vacancies anywhere, even campsites that I'd marked were apparently all full to bursting. I asked them to keep trying and hopefully something would turn up but it was starting to get desperate.

I continued on through Worthing and Shoreham almost in a daze as my mind was fixated on what I might do. Could I sleep in a shelter? On the beach, even? In my planning dreams I could, but what about in reality? Could I "*Wild camp*"? I'd never even "*Tame camped*" so that didn't look good either. I asked Nobby what we could do but he didn't come up with any answers either. To be fair, he had his mind on the road. One of us had to.

 In almost a blur I was in Hove. All of these seaside places had merged into one long promenade. Even the appearance of the sea, way back, hadn't really registered with me.

My phone rang with the dulcet guitar of "*Sultans of Swing*" by Dire Straits. This had to be good news, surely?

I stood on that seafront and listened whilst Gail told me that she had just taken a call and that my best buddy, Ed had just been rushed into hospital with a suspected heart attack. He'd had many before and he was 93 years old. She said that his family, knowing how close we were, would let her know anything when they could.

This absolutely devastated me and in my tired emotional state I stood by Nobby and I sobbed. I was totally ignorant of people walking by, just as they were about the reason for my tears. I didn't know what to do. What could I do?

Brighton seafront, promenade and cycle path was absolutely packed with tourists, ten to twenty abreast (or so it seemed). I was only able to push Nobby through the throng, following fellow pedestrianised cyclists as a snake of bikes threaded their way along.

The scene was a blur, my mind and thoughts were with my mate. Where was he now? Was he okay? How bad? I felt so helpless in this situation. I had cycled over on my bike to see him once on a Bank Holiday, just on a whim, and I found him in the early stages of one then and called the Ambulance to get him to hospital just in time, but this time I was miles away.

At last the crowds thinned and I was able to remount. I stopped again above the marina to call Gail. They still hadn't any luck finding me a resting place for the night, especially anywhere near Brighton. Obviously there were some hotels with rooms available but I was on a tight budget and not a lottery winner so they were well outside my range. The only campsite that I knew of nearby was up in the hills above Brighton and I didn't really have the legs or heart for a major climb to put a tent up. Gail said that they were full anyway.

We agreed that I would carry on for now and we would make a decision on what to do in a bit, so I plodded along the cliff tops and past the famous Roedean School. The sun was glistening on the sea now slightly behind me. The climb up the slopes was harder now. My mind was elsewhere and my heart wasn't as willing as before. The tiredness, both physical and emotional, had taken hold of this wimp and I felt that I was pedalling by memory, going through the motions a bit. I had to shake this feeling.

Looking East from Brighton Marina (still very hot)

I cycled on past Rottingdean and then down past Saltdean Lido with a great view of the white cliffs in front of me. Another harsh slow climb followed. It wasn't particularly bad but in my knacked state I struggled, but then I enjoyed a nice restful freewheel to Telscombe cliffs, then on to Peacehaven.

I stopped at Telscombe stores to get a drink and I bought some salted peanuts. A few hundred yards further on I spotted a Wimpey. I decided to stop here to phone home and see what we would decide to do.

There was no further news on Ed. The general consensus was that as I (we) couldn't find any accommodation at all anywhere within about fifteen miles, (There must have been some but we didn't know of them) there wasn't really an option of carrying on too much further.

I didn't want the trip to end this way, about a day and a half from home, but due to the fact that I had pushed myself much too hard and tried to cover far too many miles each day with an extremely heavy load without too much in the way of sensible planning, that had drained me physically and mentally without much in the form of sustenance to keep my energy levels up, I had burnt myself out.

What a sad, self-pitying, yellow bellied, disorganized wimp I had turned into!

The bad news regarding Ed was just the straw that broke the icing on the camel's back cake with a tin hat on, to mix a few metaphors there.

So, it was agreed, reluctantly, that the ride would end by Newhaven harbour. The girls would drive down to get me in a couple of hours (Jodie hadn't forgotten her words of the previous year but she couldn't leave her dad in limbo, could she?). She could have but she didn't, bless her little cotton socks.

They told me to get myself some food in the Diner and explained how to put some tracker thing on in my phone so that they could locate me or my remains. I'm surprised that they hadn't done that prior to my start! I must have been expendable then.

So I locked Nobby up outside the restaurant window and went inside. The "Duncan Norvelle" soundalike manager (You'll have to check him out on "Youfacetube" if you don't know of him. He's a 70s/80s camp comedian, and I don't mean "camp" as in tents and caravans etc.) assured me that he would be fine, and just to be sure, to be sure, as an Irishman may or may not say, I sat right beside the window, just a pane of glass between us.

I ordered a cheeseburger (another one) and chips with a large Pepsi (again, other cola's may have been available, but they may not have). Whilst awaiting my meal I asked "Duncan" to keep a watch on Nobby so that I could use the toilet facilities. This also meant that *"Duncan"* wouldn't be using the facilities at the same time. Cunning eh!

I sat there eating my burger (nowhere near as good as the earlier ones) and at first, I was feeling peeved that I'd been thwarted in my quest yet again and had, through my own stupid fault this time, failed miserably.

But there was, I admit, a slight sense of relief as I had been fretting for last couple of hours or so that I had nowhere to lay my head and now at least I knew that I'd be back in my own bed, albeit a couple of days early.

Now the pressure had eased I could concentrate on the last bit, meeting my road crew, admitting that I was a failure once more (an easy bit there) and getting home to find out how my best mate was.

Gail had called to say that the rescue party was on its way yet again (Thunderbirds are Go!) so, full of junk food, I paid and thanked *"Duncan"* and I was on my way to Newhaven. I stayed on the Cliffside path as the road was very busy and I was very tired. It was early evening in Sussex.

The road eventually parted from the sea as it steered inland for a while. On reaching a Pelican crossing for cyclists I dismounted and pushed Nobby up a steepish hill (It may have been a crossing for Pelican cyclists but I didn't see any).

At the top of the rise, through a gate and down the hill through a large housing estate I careered. The Ferry Port came into view. A Ferry appeared to be reversing back out of the harbour. Down the bottom of the hill I went alongside the River Ouse and over the bridge to our meeting place by the Ferry Port entrance.

I parked up and sat on a wall in the evening sunlight, contemplating the past few days from my journey up to Gloucester through to my ignominious ending about seventy miles short. I had travelled roughly ninety miles plus on my final day and I think that this was 30/40 miles too far.

Why did I push it so far? I just don't know, I just kept going and that wasn't the point of the trip. I hardly allowed myself any time to stand and stare, I hadn't drunk enough, I hadn't eaten enough, I hadn't seen enough, I hadn't thought things through enough. I know I keep repeating these things but it's mainly done to emphasise just how poor my planning and/or attitude was. Yes, it was a major failing, but it was also the way that I do things, a sort of "suck it and see" easy going way. That's my personality. I can't drastically alter that.

I had carted a load of camping gear across the country and not used any of it.

What a Plonker!

An hour later Jodie's little white Clio appeared beside me. There was still no news of Ed. I'd have to call in the morning. I got my usual daughterly lecture about not sulking, we loaded the car up, or rather I loaded the car up and off we went, the girls in the front thinking "*Here we go again*" and me in the back thinking "*Here we go again*".

It was a very crestfallen cyclist that arrived home that night. I had toured on my cycle so I could at least call myself a "Touring Cyclist", but I hadn't successfully completed my quest yet, and this would have to be done before I could attempt to conquer the World. It was only 300 odd miles from Wales, for Gawd's sake!

That was for the future, though, my priority now was to see how my mate was.

As it transpired, this time, thankfully Ed hadn't had a Myocardial infarction as at first thought (see, I know the correct medical terminology), but had instead contracted a very bad chest infection that still very nearly did for him. It took several weeks to shift and he had to spend some time in a Nursing home in respite before, finally being allowed back home again.

Of course, I showed my concern by blaming him entirely for my failure by being so selfish and getting rushed into hospital whilst I was away.

Blimey, you would have least thought that he would have had the decency to stay fit and well during my trip after having to endure all of the build ups for the last two plus years!

Anyone would have thought that it was boring him!

You can see how relieved I was to know he was okay. Now he would have to endure another year of planning and of talking about it. After all, he was my sound board for just about everything. I was so lucky that we had a very similar sense of humour. Not just that, I was so lucky that he was my best mate. He's not such a bad lad.

All I had to do when I got home was to get the train back up to Gloucester to collect my car. I was expecting much Mickey taking from Neil but I was surprised when he told me that he thought it was amazing that I'd got that far (over 200 miles) as I could hardly keep Nobby upright when I'd left their house.

When I left, I said that I would see them the same time next year. Andi said *"I hope that you're joking"*.

 I wasn't.

8   Once more, into the breach

In the interceding year, my hip and spine pains persisted and I was now getting pins and needles and numbness in my left foot to go along with my right side issues. I think that Hypochondria was the only ailment that I hadn't got, but I was sure that I'd catch that soon as well.

My doctor put it down to all of the cycling that I was doing. He kept encouraging me to carry on as it was really good physiotherapy for my condition and I knew that riding a bike was much more favourable to painkillers, a lot more enjoyable too.

And I had unfinished business.

My exceedingly cunning plan for my third attempt (Yes, third attempt) was to deviate away from most of my previously planned routes, and to actually book B &Bs for the end of each day so I knew that I'd have somewhere to rest my weary bones each night. This meant that I could dispense with all of the camping gear that I'd previously carted around but never actually used.

Also, I had tried camping in my back garden one night, and after watching a slug crawl up the outside of the tent and then me failing to get any sort of comfort on the hard, rough floor in my sleeping bag, I decided that, at my age, after a hard day in the saddle doing several miles, erecting a small piece of canvas like material and sharing it with all of my worldly travelling goods whilst lying in a field, was not for me.

What I'm trying to say is that I only lasted one and a half hours before moaning out loud and going back indoors at 1am to sleep in a nice warm bed. I know this because Jodie told me that she could hear me cursing prior to giving up. When the going gets tough, give up and go to bed!

The plus side to all of this meant that I wouldn't have to lug a tent, sleeping bag, pots and cooking stove across Britain. So that would make Nobby much lighter and easier to handle (in theory). I would keep the foam groundsheet as it weighed next to nothing and it would help to keep the vehicles away from me. Again, that was in theory. I never got to know if the theory worked as I left it behind in Neil's garage when I set off. Hey Ho!

I spent weeks (again) sitting at the table, planning my new route on my Ordnance Survey maps (Yep, the same ones, but cut down to save weight), this time using a different coloured highlighter pen to clearly show my exact route, avoiding major hills, dodgy main roads and un-cycle friendly areas. Again I used the CTC cycle route planner and Google Earth to visually picture the roads and any landmarks etc. What could possibly go wrong?

Both myself, and Nobby were ready. Me with my shorts, tee shirts (optimistic), waterproof jacket and trainers as before and Nobby with his new Low Rider front pannier racks and bags that I had fitted and rear panniers so that I could spread the weight around without squashing stuff (Yeah, right). I took a paperback book to help pass relaxing evenings plus wash gear and some flapjacks and some bits and bobs for the journey like bike repair stuff etc. I would obviously this time buy food from the many outlets that I would find along country lanes and in the many picturesque villages.

Prior to leaving home I had secured accommodation at four Airbnb's. This type of B&B had been recommended to me and as I was finding some B&B's very expensive when I had enquired, I took this option and thought that I'd give it a go.

For my first night on the road though I had found a room in a Pub in Bath just up from the River Avon and the Bristol/Bath cycle path. This seemed Ideal.

All I had to do now was get up to Gloucester (once more into the breach) and see my friends Andi and Neil. My plan this time was to start on a Sunday.

9   A nice fine day

Gail decided to work on Saturday morn as I was driving up to Gloucester so I took her to work at 7am then came back home to load the car. With Nobby secure on the bike rack and my bags, food and medication on board, off I went. Not even Ralph the cat was there to see me off as he had gone out looking for mice. Jodie was at a friend's so my departure from Hythe was uneventful, although I had a feeling that my successful arrival home (this time) later in the week would be slightly different. I must be a "Glass half full" person, or is it a "Glass half empty"? I don't know. It's just a glass.

The M25 was operating a "1st & 2nd gear only" day apparently, although it wasn't advertised, it did give me plenty of time to keep on checking in the mirror to look and see if the straps were loosening on Nobby. The more you look, the more you imagine disaster.

Luckily I had put a plastic freezer bag over Nobby's saddle as it started to really ploot down on the M4 all the way to Swindon then up to the fair city of GLAWSTER. I'm a massive Rugby fan, I may have mentioned it, but unfortunately, this is "my team". I've followed the Cherry & Whites for many a year through thin and thinner. You can't just change allegiance and I wouldn't want to. Remember, beauty is in the eye of the afflicted!

Anyway, I arrived safely, unloaded and had a relaxing time being ridiculed, insulted and generally ribbed again by Neil and ,again, being overly worried over by Andi. That's what good friends are for.

Before dinner, Neil took me out in his car to show me my route from his house, through the streets to join the Sharpness Canal tow path by Sainsbury. It seemed pretty straight forward, from the

Abbeydale area where they lived, past Tredworth cemetery, across the Bristol Road, and "Voila".

Although I must at this point state that my eyes were scrunched firmly closed and my fingernails embedded into the plastic dashboard as Neil wasn't the slowest driver in Gloucester, in fact I'm not totally convinced that his car, a Ford Getouttheway, had a brake pedal at all. My feet were the only ones, it seemed, that were pushing down hard on imaginary pedals!

I had quite a fretful night thinking about what may lay ahead and rose before 7am. After bathroom ablutions and a breakfast of tea and toast (a bit of butter would have been nice), I was ready to load up Nobby and be on my way. Once all (apart from the foam mat) was loaded, I bid my mates a hearty farewell for the second year running and headed off into the grey damp morning.

I found Sainsbury without too much trouble as it was quiet on this Sunday morning. Following the Gloucester & Sharpness Canal it should have been impossible to get lost, you could only go Southerly or Northerly and I was heading South.

The tow path went alongside an Industrial estate at first, down towards Quedgeley, and then the first spots of rain got progressively heavier, making me stop to rummage around in my panniers for my waterproof jacket. This wasn't a very promising start to the ride as the wind was also reasonably strong and into my face as well, the dark clouds heading directly towards me.

The canal side path was more suited to mountain bikes, unpaved with large stone chippings and certainly not Ideal for a laden Nobby with thinner smoother tyres. It was a bit disconcerting astride a loaded bike on an uneven stony path next to a wide, deep ship canal, cycling into driving wind and rain, but as I kept telling myself (again) *"You chose to do this so get on with it and enjoy!"*

Well, you can only take so much of this enjoyment on a wet Sunday morn, so I left the canal near Hardwicke and headed along a lane to Longney. Although the rain was constant now, it was easy riding and my excitement jolted at my first sight of the River Severn, which I found myself cycling alongside, only separated by some trees and bushes.

Nobby at the Anchor Inn with Lenny who I kept in the panniers as he got soaked through (then I forgot about him)

At the Anchor Inn Public House at Epney I stopped to take some photos from the riverside along a sweeping wide bend, looking over to the Forest of Dean in the distance on the far side. Yes, this was definitely part of my dream, despite the rain.

Passing Frampton on Severn, I again followed the canal as far as Slimbridge, just Nobby and me pootling through the Gloucestershire countryside, passing farms and fields and listening out for the distant village church bells.

I caught the aroma of a flock of pigs in a small field long before I saw them. Why is it that they wait until a pig has died before they cure it! Anyway, this flock were all *"Gloucester Old Spots"* and there was a gaggle of sheep in the next field. I knew my country upbringing would benefit me on this trip!

Crossing the Sharpness canal

The sun was making a stuttering appearance through the grey clouds when I reached Berkeley, it was here that I made my first major error of the day. After cruising along meandering lanes all morning, keeping well out of reach of the notorious A38, I took a wrong turning after consulting my new highlighted route on the map and found myself somehow cycling on the A38.

This was not good, not good at all.

Checking the map again I saw a way out at the village of Stone so I pedalled on. I now had a choice, I could stay on this Hellish road down to Alveston or I could turn off and head for the Severn Bridge which was my initial intention, as I wanted this trip to, again be from Wales.

So I turned off. More little villages and hamlets and country lanes later, with, now good views over the Severn and Wales, despite the gloomy skies and intermittent rain I reached the bridge and I just cycled over.

It felt a bit weird and not so fulfilling this time as I was only doing this to reach the *"Welcome to Wales"* sign *"Croeso I Gymru"* again, and turn round after taking a picture and cycle straight back across again into England.

 Well it would have been easy had it not been for the wind, although not too strong it was blowing, both across and towards me from the Right. Not a headwind as such but enough to make me pedal a bit harder.

This time I hadn't bothered to take my recorder as it wasn't very secure in its holder and I didn't have a very good track record at actually recording stuff with it, did I?

After last year's epic climb (for me) pushing Nobby up the hill after Tockington, I instead headed to Elberton, then at Alveston I crossed the dreaded A38 for what, thankfully would be the last time.

At this point, whilst traversing a bridge over the M5 the thunder started. Rumbling at first in the distant South West, getting nearer, and then directly overhead. As the sky darkened to a deep shade of navy blue I stopped to put my flashing headlight and rear light on (I had kept them within easy reach this time). Although they made me feel a bit more visible to traffic I was, I admit, frequently aided by flashes of lightning bringing all too brief shafts of daylight onto what must have looked a pitiful sight.

My inward questioning thought as to why it was so dark was partially interrupted and answered by a massive hailstone shower that temporally turned the road white. With just hedges either side of the lane, there was nothing that I could do other than keep pedalling whilst showing off a false nonchalant appearance to the bemused drivers and their passengers in their vehicles by whistling and singing to myself *"Raindrops keep falling on my head"*.

They were more like golf balls really!

It kept me alert and going and I felt that it was better than crying anyway. The hailstorm stopped as quickly as it started and the sun came out as if somebody had switched a light on, to glisten off the many puddles now formed at the side of the lane.

At a place called *"Frogland Cross"* Honest! Instead of following my route marked to Frampton Cotterell I inadvertently deviated once more by continuing South, passing over the M4 then the M32 through Hambrook and up near Frenchay Hospital when I spotted a sign for Downend.

Ah Ha! This I remembered from a year ago, and before you could chuck a yoghurt at a goose, I found myself on the Bristol/Bath Railway Cycleway. I allowed myself an *"Oh Yes!"* and had the smug look of somebody who knew exactly where he was and where he was going.

It was only briefly though, as I started to cycle towards Bristol before realizing my error after 200m. I pretended to check my phone so that anyone passing wouldn't notice my abrupt about turn. So much for looking smug.

Once my minor blip was sorted, I was off down and around several little bends and heading towards Bath. It was now around 4.30/5pm so I phoned the New Crown Inn, where I was staying to say that I would be there sometime soon. The Landlady seemed delighted that I'd made it so far (I had told them previously where I was cycling from) although what she actually said was that both her and her husband (The Landlord) were soon going out to visit his mum, which they did every Sunday (Ah nice!) but that they would leave the yard gate open for me if they had gone so that I could put Nobby in and then we could lock him in their garage when they had got back and put their car in.

Pedalling a bit quicker to try to reach the pub before they left, I was being thwarted by the wind and rain which had started again and now had become a constant companion.

My next mistake was to spot a sign for Bath Spa University, I believe, so I left the cycleway, pedalled up a zig zag stone chipped cycle path to a point somewhere along the main road between Bath and Bristol. I'm sure that it must have been tiredness that made me think that I'd reached my destination. This was nowhere near anywhere, so I back tracked (yet again) to the cycleway and carried on into Bath alongside the River Avon.

I now actually knew where I was, and after a few more miles I turned off the river by a college and I could virtually see the pub up at the top of Chelsea Hill. I'm afraid that I had no strength left to ride Nobby up the hill so I pushed through the rain and arrived at the pub just as the Landlord/Landlady were getting into their car. They viewed me with a look that bordered on pity , said that I had cycled a

Hell of a way (I already knew that), just to put my bike in, go and see the barmaid for my room key, get a nice hot shower and relax now. They would be back later. I liked these people!

Surely nowt could go wrong now that I'd arrived, tired but safe. After locking Nobby to a table under cover from the rain I went into the bar with all of my gear to get my key. I got a few good humoured comments from the bar folk like *"Wet out, is it?"* and *"Been swimming, have ya?"* I took it all in the smiley spirit that it was given, and dripped all over the carpet whilst the barmaid searched for my key.

I was given, not only my room key, but an almost identical one for the bathroom that was conveniently situated opposite my room. On reaching my room, and a very pleasant room it was, my first job was to put my trainers out on the window ledge to dry out as the rain now had stopped (Sod's law) and the sun was out.

Lenny having a sleep at the pub (still soaking wet)

Having a nice cuppa

And finally, trying to dry out in my sopping wet training shoe

When Lenny had dried out, he went to sleep in my rear pannier and he slept all the way (Well, you couldn't have me talking about him as if he was real, could you?).

Nobby wouldn't have liked it either!

After getting my wash bag and clean tee shirt, shorts etc. I grabbed the key and headed for the bathroom for that well earned (I thought) long hot shower. It was grand.

I scooped up all of my things, ablutions over, to take back to my room when I realized that I only had the bathroom key. My room key was on the sideboard, locked safely inside the room.

Oh Poohy!

There then followed a rather sheepish (though very clean) embarrassed cyclist going down to the bar where I had to explain to all and sundry in the small room what had happened. The barmaid, bless her, took a large bunch of keys up to the door to try, alas with no luck, so she made a quick call to the Landlady's mobile and was told where the spare key was. No worries!

I thought that at this stage I should make a discrete exit (With my room key) 50m down the hill to the local Spar shop to stock up with some evening supplies, nibbles etc. On sneaking back to my room, avoiding the bar and sniggers, I noticed that I had several missed calls from Andi in Gloucester so I phoned her up.

 "I've been worried sick" she said *"You left hours ago and we haven't heard a word from you, we thought you'd had an accident or something"* I assured her that I was okay and all was fine and I briefly ran through the past few hours. I promised that I would check in with them every night. I think that Neil uttered *"Oh Whoopy Doo!"* He's a cheerful little fellow.

After I put the phone down, Penny, the Landlady (Her husband was called Kelvin) knocked on my door and asked if I wanted to pay her now as I wanted to leave early in the morn before they were up. That was also the reason for me not having a cooked breakfast although cereals and milk were provided in the room (The milk was in a little fridge) so I would have those instead.

I duly paid for the room, apologized for the key incident and that was the last that I saw of anybody at the pub as, after I moved Nobby to the garage for the night, I stayed in my room listening to the now gently falling rain over the city of Bath, reading as I was so shattered after over ten hours on the road and seventy plus miles in all weathers (almost).

I checked in with home, all was fine there. In fact I think that they were happy that I was on my way, also I think that they were happy that they had some peace and quiet as well. I lay on the bed and was vaguely aware of the Sunday night revellers making their way home and gradually dozed off.

10 There's always another Hill....

I woke to the sight of drizzle on the window but after a quick shower, remembering to take both keys with me this time, some cereal, tea and packing of panniers, the fine rain had stopped. I went down to the yard, got Nobby out of the garage that he was placed in last night, I loaded up, pushed the keys through the letterbox as instructed then I was off.

I was astride my trusty bike at first, then pushing him through the city centre, looking for a café which I never found.

Finally, after checking out Bath's Rugby ground (again) from across the river, I crossed Poultney Bridge heading towards Sydney Gardens and the Kennett &Avon then, before my very eyes, was a café.

I parked Nobby on his stand and strode into the establishment. *"Two bacon rolls please"* I stated firmly with much jolliness.

The man looked at me as if I had just dropped out of a dog's bottom and told me in a snooty condescending voice *"Sorry we don't do processed meat here, try back in the town"*

I was almost speechless (not quite though) *"This is a café, surely?"*

He just stared.

"Forget it" I muttered to nobody in particular and traipsed back out, I unparked Nobby and headed off yonder, to the canal.

"Bugger" I said to Nobby. *"I was looking forward to that. I'll get brekkies at the café at Bradford on Avon, onwards!"* Nobby didn't reply which I thought was a tad rude of him. Ne'er mind.

After last year, this part of the journey was familiar. A push up the steps from Sydney Gardens to the canal, this time I pointed Left instead of Right and skedaddled off along a quite puddly towpath. The greyness of the early morning gradually lifted to be replaced by mugginess as the sun tried to force its way through.

"C'mon Sun" I called out without realizing that I was being observed by some canal folk breakfasting on their narrow boat. *"Morning"* they called out as I waved back, almost toppling into the brown murk as I did. They could have invited me over, I could smell bacon, for crying out loud!

Come to think of it, I do tend to call out things, totally oblivious of my surroundings especially if I spy a solitary Magpie. *"Good morning Mr. Magpie, How's the wife?"* I enquire each time. Fortunately I think that this is my only superstitious chant

"Touch Wood".

I must confess that this year's cycle along the Kennett & Avon wasn't as exciting and enjoyable as last year's jaunt, possibly because it was all new then and something that I'd always wanted to do, also the weather was glorious then in the late afternoon. Now, it's early to midmorning, damp but warming up. I'm seeing things totally differently this time and, as with the Severn Bridge, it's something that I'd already done so it's all a little bit anticlimactic. The two aqueducts, Dundas and Avoncliff are just landmarks to tick off and to pass by this time.

So I was glad that from Semington onwards I'd chosen and highlighted on my maps a much more rural and different route (Oh yeah, we'll see about that!).

The café at Bradford on Avon duly arrived with a disappointment that they only had cakes on offer to eat, and very expensive they were as well so I gave them a miss, took out a bank loan and had a cup of coffee instead. Still no food apart from my flapjack snacks.

As it got warmer I decided to take off my rare British Lions lightweight windcheater and wrap it over my handlebars in case I needed it later on. (There is a point to this paragraph so bear with me).

Further on, around Hilperton marina I met a young chap on a bike towing a trailer with his young toddler son in, plus camping gear on board and his elder son on his bike alongside. He said that they were heading to Newbury, and then on to London and camping on the way and that they were really enjoying it, despite the temperamental weather, which I thought was absolutely brilliant. This was what it was all about really. Getting out there and doing it, even when it gets hard and, perhaps not so enjoyable.

This was my new mantra since last year's fiasco, *"Tough times don't last. Tough folk do!"* well, we'll see about that. I may be tested at some time in the week, but surely not today. Today would be a good day.

Anyway, I passed the bridge leading to Semington village and carried on to the small swing bridge a bit further on where I rejoined the canal last year. This time I would be leaving the canal by this bridge, no need to do the Caen Flight and Devizes again. This time I had planned it differently, and better.

Over the swing bridge I went and up to the gate leading to the lane. As I climbed onto Nobby again I thanked the canal for another safe, carefree journey without any problems or hitches. With thanks said, I pushed down on the pedals, whereupon my favourite rare British Lions windcheater fell from the handlebars and got caught up in the chain, jamming it against the front cogs.

Nobby came to a sudden stop sending me forwards against my low Hybrid crossbar, causing some discomfort in the undercarriage region which could have been a lot worse with a higher crossbar.

I pulled the, now oil blackened, ripped top from the chain with a look of total disbelief. I may have even shouted *"Blast it"* or *"Pickled scrumpings"* or some other non-abusive curse. I am a nice person, after all.

Although my top was ruined I still decided to put it into my panniers and carry it home, possibly hoping for sympathy from the family, but mainly because I couldn't bear to part with it, even in its destroyed state.

Is that sad or what?

Oh well, Hey Ho, onwards I go.

I only had to follow the A361 to Devizes for a short distance where I turned off for Potterne and Urchfont. Unfortunately I turned off to the Right for the village of Keevil before realizing my mistake and back tracking through Bulkington and Worton to muddle my way in my usual haphazard fashion to Potterne.

I couldn't believe how hilly it seemed to be, every way that I turned. I had to push Nobby up so many lumpy country lanes.

The "George & Dragon" pub where I crossed the A360 at Potterne (not for long though)

The "George & Dragon" pub where I crossed the A360 at Potterne (not for long though)

On my arrival (eventually) in Potterne I met the A360. I had to cross it to take a bridleway on to Urchfont to cut a chunk off the route, cunning eh?

No, not really as, after pushing up a steep little lane, the lane ran out to be replaced by a thick muddy path that I couldn't even start to get through. It was like thick chocolate custard with puddles in it, and that is the definite polite description.

So it was back to the A360, up a long hill (again) until I could turn off through Potterne Wick and onwards to the elusive Urchfont. This was the real countryside with real country lanes with many rises, there were some descents as well but the rises were really holding me up and tiring me out, as without a bike I can find walking quite difficult, but as I might have said before. I don't complain!

I finally reached Urchfont and went into the local village store at the Lamb Inn. After spending a while scouring around for provisions all that I managed to purchase was a bunch of bananas….. Oh Ho!!!! NANA ALERT! NANA ALERT!

Oh yes, and one apple.

There were no pies or pastries at all, and do you know how heavy a bunch of bananas are?

I didn't but I soon found out!

I thought that I must eat the bananas before I got to Salisbury as the weight wouldn't help my poor legs. Also, I didn't want another incident.

By now I had decided, despite my vow to myself not to, to take the A342 between Devizes and Amesbury as per last year as I kept getting lost in the winding roller coaster country lanes. I couldn't blame the maps or my marked out route (Yes I could).

The maps didn't show the hilly bits but Google Earth would have shown them, I think that I just missed them (So, my fault again).

I just wished that I could have kept to the route but I couldn't because I was a feeble wimp... er ...probably. So the decision had been made, and halfway through the day I pedalled on, my dream of cycling right over Salisbury Plain following tank tracks on a public right of way was now..... Just a dream.

I would still come out at Amesbury, albeit by an already ridden boring, not to mention dodgy, main road. I needed a change of luck.

At a junction in Urchfont, I got pointed in the right direction (I thought) by a chap who told me to turn to the Right

"You don't want to go Left, that's to Devizes" he said, so off I went, as he said that I would reach the main road a bit further down.

I passed through Eastcott and Easterton and Market Lavington to turn Left onto the main road at West Lavington. I was pootling along merrily eating my apple when it occurred to me that none of this was at all familiar.

I stopped, finished my apple, I think it was a Cox's French Golden Pippin, and checked my trusted and extremely accurate map. It then became as clear as a new piece of cling film that my first choice initial planned route across Salisbury Plain, tank tracks and all, was about four miles to the East of me, but more alarmingly, the road that I'd chosen only half an hour ago, the A342 was a further six or so miles further East than that.

How could I have got it so wrong?

Twice?

Where did I take the wrong turning?

Where the heck was I heading to now?

And, perhaps an even more important question to ask?

Where the hell was I?

Well, my unflappable map reading ability had placed me on the A360. At least I was heading in the correct general direction (I think). There was no point in turning back as who's to say that I may have taken a slight detour again and then Gawd knows where I could've ended up.

So along the A360 I went, cutting a path through Salisbury Plain on a slightly wider road than was anticipated. At least on a main road, I thought, nothing else could go wrong!

I pedalled along a casual downhill section, picking up some speed as I entered the town of Tilshead when....... My back wheel all of a sudden felt all wobbly and sluggish.

A puncture!

I couldn't believe it, "*I don't believe it!*" I cried. There, see I told you I couldn't believe it. Just as it seemed that the journey was getting a tadge easier, although on a busy A road, the little Elf of cycle mishaps had grabbed a wet haddock and slapped me in the face with it.

I found a piece of grass near the village hall, took everything from Nobby's racks and set fire to the lot!

No I didn't.

Only joshing. I turned Nobby upside down and proceeded to slowly replace the damaged tube with a brand new one. I carried two spares so that I didn't have to fix any puncture there and then.

I decamped on the grass on the right

I took ages to get the tyre back on as it was a very tight 32 inch one and I was now very hot, very sweaty, very oily and very tired.

Eventually I got all of the gear (unburnt) back onto the bike and after a chat with a very nice and jovial retired ex-cyclist Scotsman (I don't know what he said!) I was again on my way, although my back wheel did feel a teensy weensy bit wobbly and not running true, Hmmmm!

I trundled on over more undulating scenery on the Plain down to Shrewton. I was a tad disappointed not to spot any Shrews going about their business but, Hey Ho.

Through the Shrewless village of Shrewton and onwards I went, I should have headed on the A344, then onto country lanes to Amesbury where I had spent a lot of time in preparation working out a cunning route out of the town, much different to last year, by using a cycle path up to spooky Porton Down and then a straight forward route on to my Airbnb on the South East side of Salisbury.

Instead of the much researched way that I've just mentioned, I turned Right to stay on the A360 as I had spotted a sign for Salisbury and it seemed, at that time, a good Idea to stick with the road that I was on. What could possibly go wrong with that? As I neared a mini roundabout I was afforded a good view to the East where, over the quite stunning rolling hills, all that I could see was stationary traffic. Oh!

I zoomed over from Right to Left at this roundabout (Yeah right, I did!). This isn't my picture! If it was, you wouldn't see the road for stationary traffic.

I was approaching the intersection with the A303 by Stonehenge. Nice one, Hawkeye!

How did this happen?

Where were my nice quiet country lanes?

Luckily as the traffic was at a virtual standstill I managed to thread my way through. I must confess to feeling slightly smug for once as, on this now, scorching hot late afternoon, I was able to carry on pedalling whilst others were shut in their little tin boxes waiting patiently to move on.

Any inward gloating that I may have felt was quickly knocked on the head when I saw how narrow this fast two lane highway was with more ups and downs than a hyper active Yo-Yo on steroids. It was, at times, very scary, especially when I had to get off and push Nobby up the steeper (and sometimes even, not so steeper) bits. There was no footpath nor anywhere to go other than forwards, keeping in as tight as I could to the verge and hope for understanding motorists, 99% of drivers gave me room if they had to either stop or slow down to pass me for which I was eternally grateful.

Two chaps in a Land Rover even asked if I was okay or needed a lift up one particular narrow inclined section. I thanked them but told them that I was okay although a very tiny bit knacked, they smiled, waved good luck and carried on their way. That gave me a spur and helped me to keep going.

I finally reached the Western edge of Salisbury (the wrong side) early evening and muddled my way across and through the streets. I asked a lady who was unloading her car if she knew of the address I was heading for, she informed me that it was only a couple of roads away (How did that happen?). She gave me directions that even I managed to follow and I arrived, seventy odd miles and almost eleven hours later at my Airbnb.

My host was Pamella and her husband Micheal (The double of retired Rugby referee Tony Spreadbury, my favourite all-time referee) sorry non Rugby folk, of which Micheal was one.

They were absolutely brilliant in every way. Coffee was taken on the patio after I had locked Nobby safely in the shed. They had two other guests staying from Australia and they were all very courteous and polite in listening to my traumas from the day and provided me with tissues when I burst into uncontrollable sobbing as I recalled the events (that bit isn't true). They didn't have any tissues.

After a glorious power shower, change of clothes and phone calls to both Gail and Andi, when I had to explain again and again where I had gone wrong this time to much tutting and sniggering (not very supportive), it was time for me to relax in my room, work out where, exactly I had gone wrong as I didn't entirely believe my version that I'd given to my cheerleaders (Hmph!), and there were too many instances to explain to them anyway, eat some snacks that I had got on the way, no bananas this time, I had eaten them all.

I'm not stupid, well I am stupid but not when it comes to mushy nanas now, I've learned the hard way, and have a little quiet chill out read of my book.

I really did need to sort out my food intake and eat properly. This was easier said than done whilst using mainly back roads but I had hardly seen owt on the main roads either, but I did need to make a better effort.

There, that's told me off.

11 Oh it's hot, hot, hot!

After a good night's sleep there was no problem with eating first thing in the morning as Micheal provided a brilliant feast of a full breakfast, even almost force feeding me extra sausages to get me off to a great start. Cereal, toast, orange juice and tea followed meaning that Nobby had a heavier load to carry.

I checked the back wheel again but although it was still a bit wobbly running, I couldn't figure out why.

After receiving directions for the first bit from my host (The best, nicest B&B I have stayed in) I was off on my travels once again.

Day three had begun and my destination was Emsworth, just past Havant in Hampshire. Once again I had my route all marked out. Surely today I would be able to keep to it.

It was another hot summer's day. My first task was to cross the busy A36 to the village of Alderbury. I crossed at a place called Petersfinger, I never did see the rest of him.

I asked a lady walking her dog, just to double check, if I was on the correct road to Alderbury. She said *"It is, but I'm afraid it's uphill"* It was, and so, fully laden with breakfast, I got off Nobby and slowly pushed.

Through Alderbury and back over the A36 again and along the B roads to East Grimstead, West Dean, East Tytherley and Lockerly then down to Romsey.

This was, at last the sort of cycling that I had hoped for. It was even impossible for me to go astray this time. I cruised along under blue sky and warm sunshine with hardly a breath of wind. The road signs were easy to follow with only slight undulations in the countryside and pretty villages along the way.

At a railway level crossing, the gate was down and I got into a brief conversation with two elderly Dutch cyclists who told me that they were cycling back to Harwich, and then home. They were totally kitted out with full panniers like my own, except they looked more adept at using all of the kit that they had. I, on the other hand, couldn't even read a map properly (it has been alleged) and I also had problems in setting my Fit Bit watch each day (I don't think that Jodie explained it fully to me, but I won't let on!).

The Dutchies or Nederlanders said that they were enjoying their trip and they seemed like nice folk, though a little serious in their manner. Perhaps they didn't really want to talk to me as they were riding as a pair. I was different in that respect, as I was on my Todd I would chat to anyone, especially if I was lost and needed help and directions.

It did also become apparent that people were, in general, more willing to talk to me, that's the bonus of being a solo cyclist I think, either that or I looked in such state, lost and in pain or despair, that they all felt sorry for me. But let's not go with that train of thought. I am a nice, approachable, friendly soul who exudes warmth and charm (Hopefully nobody that knows me will read this!).

Anyway, it didn't make no never mind because the two Dutch Elders pedalled off at a quick pace as soon as the train passed. I kept them at a short distance until they stopped at a village shop. I was going to stop for supplies but instead I decided to get ahead of them and, hopefully, stay ahead as it would have been embarrassing to have them overtake me as if I was an asthmatic Walrus on a power walk.

Luckily this didn't happen. I must have either been going too fast for them (I did reach 14mph at one point) or, more likely, they were still at the shop having an early lunch.

As I reached the junction of the A3057 by Stoneymarsh I could have turned Left to King's Somborne, approximately six miles to the North, but as I'd already gone via there last year, remembering the long uphill sections over Farley Mount, I turned Right, on my planned route down to Romsey.

I don't know whether it was the heat of the day now or what it was but Romsey passed by in a blur. I was through the town and on the road to North Baddesley.

I was on the A27. Well, actually mostly on a cycle path alongside the A27. It was straightforward through the edge of Chilworth, over the M27, and then I got lost.

I was intending, on my planned route, to find the A33 down into Southampton and across the River Itchen, then cycle to the River Hamble alongside Southampton Water. In an Ideal world that is what would have happened, but in my world, with the sun beating down, surrounded by snarling cars, vans, buses and trucks, I was blundering my way along, trying to keep beside, or near to the A27 which was only approximately four miles from my highlighted pathway.

The countryside had all but gone now as I pedalled on with not much of a clue as to where I was going until I crossed the River Hamble near Bursledon. I had a great view over a marina on both sides of the bridge. It was time for a brief stop and a drink and a flapjack while I rechecked the map once again.

I wasn't actually too far from my chosen course, just a couple of miles, so I decided to carry on to Fareham. I was surrounded by boats and boating paraphernalia, chandlery's etc. The sun was beating down and I felt that I was near the coast at last. Blimey, there appeared to be some money in this area.

A slight rise in the road now for a bit with, at first, a cycle lane and when that ran out I used the path as it was a lot safer than the road with some large trucks edging past.

I know that bikes shouldn't be on the footpaths, but if you're polite and give way to pedestrians then most folk don't seem to object, especially if you smile a greeting to them and explain that it's much safer on the path than *"Out there with the maniacs"* I've had quite a few chuckles back and *"I don't blame you"* replies.

Just be considerate and be ready to apologize. Life is so much easier with a smile.

It was far too hot to rush anyway. In fact, despite my radar going awry, it was turning into the best day of the ride. Now I decided that I had to get the back wheel checked and to get some food.

The last section into Fareham was on a dual carriageway so as soon as I could I was back on the path.

It doesn't make you any less of a touring cyclist by riding this way. Do what you feel safe with. I wished that I'd had a path yesterday from Stonehenge down to Salisbury but C'est la vie!

And I don't even think that my left behind bedding roll would have given me any solace either.

I cycled past the Railway station and found a bike shop, Solent Cycles on West Street. The chaps in there were great. They gave the wheel a good spin and checked Nobby for any problems. They couldn't spot any issues with the wheel. It was just a quick once over, I know, lasting only a few brief minutes but it was reassuring to know that all was okay.

I even got some approving and, dare I say, admiring comments on my journey which really perked me up and made me feel good (and I defy anyone to not feel the same, so there!). Confidence boosted, it was time to get myself some nosh.

I only travelled about 200m past Aldi, on my Right, and I found myself outside Café Ethos. This establishment was absolutely perfect. I parked Nobby just outside the door by a window, went in and ordered two bacon rolls and a coke (This time it may have been any brand, I'm not telling).

It felt so good as I sat by the window watching the world go by, actually eating food instead of just thinking about it. To be honest it was indeed so good that I asked for a third bacon roll and another (unnamed) coke. I felt so recharged after this relaxing repast that I phoned home to let them know. It was nice to report on good news for a change and I knew that they'd be pleased to know it.

I sat in the window where the blackboards are placed, with Nobby outside

I actually think that they were pleased to know that I was still going. The really nice Chinese café owner was so obliging that he watched over Nobby for me so that I could use his toilet facilities.

Fully refreshed, I remounted my trusty steed and mooched off in an Easterly direction past Porchester where I came into contact with the sea once more, well the bit known as Portsmouth Harbour anyway, looking South over to Gosport and Portsmouth.

As you can see, it was a lovely day now and a great view

As I continued I looked Left and up to Ports Down and the viewpoint where I had my superb burgers last year. I knew that I was getting near to Havant now. I just had to keep going as I was and all would be Tickety Boo.

I had now rejoined the B2177 into Havant, an old friend from last year, although I couldn't remember this actual bit. I stopped in an area that must have been called Belmont as I went into *"Belmont News"* shop and bought a super cool orange ice lolly. I sat in the shade on the grass verge to enjoy it. And enjoy it I did.

I double checked my map, I didn't seem to have a marked route through Havant so it was just *"Suck it and see"* again, like last time, and hope for the best. With luck, I'd remember bits.

I worked my way through Havant quite easily considering I had no Idea which way or where I was going.

Meandering along the good old A259 again (my kind of road), I found myself around Emsworth. After cycling around for a while trying to get my bearings (What bearings?) I approached a couple of likely looking folk to ask for directions.

Well you know what they say? *"If you want to know the time, ask a Policeman"* or is it *"If you want to know the way, ask a Policeman and a lady Police Community Support Officer"*?

So I did, and the two young Whippersnappers (both looked of school age to me, but it was the holidays) confidently directed me on my way to my Airbnb in Victoria Road, so off I went, beside a large school with construction work going on, all fenced off along a cycle path, where I felt (in fact I was sure) that I'd followed their implicit instructions to the letter, crossing the level crossing at the local train station, I soon found myself looking at ….. Countryside! Oh dear!

I persevered for a bit then did an about turn, crossing back over the crossing that I'd crossed over only some minutes before, only this time, feeling crosser.

I spotted P.C. & W.P.C.P.C.S.O. Haven't a clue patrolling along the road ahead. Before they saw me and quite possibly thought me a fool, or even arrested me for wasting Police and Police Community Support Officers time, I quickly skedaddled down a side street, and after a while of aimlessly pedalling around I found a One Stop shop back on the main road.

I stopped at the shop, that's the One Stop shop, went into the shop to restock my provisions for my evening feast, and to once again request directions to my overnight location.

The girl behind the counter didn't even know of the road! WHAT?????

So off I went again, this time for a change, I got lucky and I found the right road, albeit at the wrong end, and so I sauntered along it until I reached my destination for the night.

As I knocked the door a man in old overalls answered it

"G'day Kev"

Ah ha! An Aussie, I correctly assumed. I'm good at that sort of thing. He was also called Kev (Obviously a good choice), and without resorting to stereotyping people, both him and his wife Sue (who I met in the morn) were a real couple of bonzer folk. They made me feel so welcome in their home which, once inside, resembled a very upmarket Tardis, all of the work was done by Kev, himself, and I must say that it was all done to such a high standard, much too good for the likes of me and Nobby, but Kev didn't think so, he even gave Nobby his own room (Well, large Utility room) Top man.

As I sat enjoying a welcome cup of tea with Kev, he informed me that, as I'd had such a brilliant hot sunny day's cycling today, tomorrow's forecast was for persistent heavy rain from early morning till after lunch time. He did try not to smile as he told me (but he failed) and, on seeing my despondent face with eyes welling up, he lightened the report by telling me that any wind would be in my favour! Oh deep joy.

Hey Ho, whatever the score with the weather I had to do the miles to Rottingdean, to the East of Brighton, regardless so I just accepted that I might get slightly damp.

How little did I know?

In the meantime, after a long day in the sun and sixty to seventy odd miles (I didn't check properly on my bike computer or my Fitbit) it was time for a well earned shower, then feet up, eat my snacks (no nana's again) and then night nights.

It was starting to get dark when I made my way along the corridor to the bathroom. I opened the door in the gloom. No light switch! Where was it? I didn't want to troop back downstairs to ask about something that I expected to be blatantly obvious so I fumbled around in the semi darkness for several minutes until I finally realized that it was a modern switch that blended in with its surroundings, what I wasn't expecting though, was that it would actually be situated outside the bathroom in the corridor. I didn't mention it to Kev. He may have called me a drongo!

12 Was That Noah? ....

I was woken by the sound of rain lashing against the window, so I got up, had a shower, though why I bothered when I'd get a good one soon anyway I don't know. I got all of my gear together and went down to the kitchen to make a cuppa. Kev and Sue were both up and they introduced me to their son who was staying for a couple of days from Bristol.

Although breakfast wasn't offered in the Airbnb booking, they kindly invited me to join them with toast, marmalade and even Vegemite if I wanted it, which I did. After watching the updated forecast (it wasn't good) and a bit of a yarn, it was time to depart. I couldn't have been made to feel anymore welcome at their house. Good on ya both.

As Kev wouldn't give me a lift to Brighton (only joshing) I bade them farewell and Nobby splashed off through the puddles to the main road. I kept to the road as much as felt safe but when the road narrowed I took to the path. Southbourne and Broadbridge were passed without me looking up or around too much as any potholes were hidden in the puddles.

I found myself aquaplaning through Chichester. At least my waterproof jacket was doing its job really well and there was no point, I felt, donning waterproof trousers as it's not very pleasant cycling in them, anyway I'd discovered that I'd been given waterproof skin and it wasn't cold, so onwards.

Somehow without really noticing, Chichester was behind me, I had just concentrated on the roads and traffic and managing to stay on the bike, so to be back on the A259 making towards Bognor was just blending into the greyness and wetness of the morning (Did I mention it was raining?).

I didn't want to pedal but I didn't want to stop. This was one time when my mantra about tough times and tough folk was at its most potent, although *"fine words doth butter no parsnips"* whatever that may mean.

There was nowt to see in the, now, torrential rain so it was time for me to start singing. At least it looked to the passing motorists that I was oblivious to the conditions and, possibly even, enjoying it (in my mind, anyway).

There was no point in being miserable or breaking down into uncontrollable sobbing so it was best to smile and to give a cheery *"Good Morning"* to any other poor souls getting saturated like myself. One lady actually laughed when I said *"We could do with a bit more rain"* as I squelched past her.

With visibility now down to just the near surrounding area there didn't seem to be much point in heading for the seafront to admire the briny view so I paddled.... Er... I mean pedalled on through the town and back out past some fields to the A259.

This must have been the scariest bit of the road so far, even worse than the section down to Salisbury, as it was just a single lane each way fast stretch and I hugged the edge as best I could. With my bike lights flashing, I hoped that the whizzing past traffic would see me in time in the rain and gloom and be patient and give me a wide berth.

I knew that if I caused any accident involving a truck carrying tortoises and another carrying terrapins, it could have been a turtle disaster!

Please forgive me for that one.

At Climping a footpath appeared and I was up and on it before you could say Boo to a grouse! (We don't like to frighten geese in Kent). I had never been so grateful to pedal along a path and to get off that road.

At a large roundabout the path widened to become a cycle path as well. Things were looking up, although I still wasn't looking up as I would get an eye full of precipitation that made me look like I was crying, and I wasn't because I'm a brave little soldier. At least my hair was getting a good wash.

This, at the moment, was the best riding of the day so far, even in the downpour I thought that things could and would only get better. I just needed to keep my mind switched on.

Have you ever wondered why Tarzan never had a beard?

I just needed to keep my mind switched on.

I stopped on the bridge over the River Arun and looked at my bike computer to see how far I'd travelled so far today. 00.00 miles. Water had obviously got in and mashed up the works. Oh Toadstools!!

My poor little bike computer

I'd had that computer for ages and it had never let me down. Mind you, I'd never ridden through one long continuous puddle in a monsoon before, so perhaps I should have wrapped a sandwich bag over it for protection. After all I'd still got the bag protection on the saddle from the journey up to Gloucester. No point now. Horses, bolts and stable doors spring to mind. My fault entirely!

I did have a back up computer somewhere in my panniers but it was unlikely that I would start rummaging now.

We had a vote and unanimously decided that I desperately needed a break as it was now mid morning (actually, I decided. Nobby kept quiet, I think he was sulking as I wouldn't buy him any water wings).

I'd done quite well considering. I'd done really well considering that I was soaked from the waist down. My jacket was working superbly but all of the water was running down onto my shorts. The kitchen roll and tissues in my pockets had all turned to mush.

My sugar free fruit sweets had leaked their entire colour and were now all sticky bland clear sweeties (it was fun guessing which one I was sucking though).

The cycle path had gone and it was back to the edge of the road as I crawled into Littlehampton (stop it!) town centre. I found a pedestrian precinct which was almost devoid of pedestrians (due to the weather, perhaps).

A GREGGS !!!!!

I found a Greggs and ordered a bacon roll, for a change and a cardboard cup of tea to warm me up even though I wasn't cold. I then sat outside at a table under some awning out of most of the rain where I could pull Nobby up next to me as he was wet as well.

It was tiring cycling in the rain. I suppose you could say that I was yawning under the awning that morning. It would be childish to do so though.

It was a most welcome break but I was soon eager to be on the move again so off I toddled, through the precinct, it was full of charity shops manned by volunteers, I wouldn't do voluntary work if you paid me!

I was then out onto a one way system that I enjoyed so much that I went around twice before spilling back out onto the main road (I'm fed up with saying A259 now).

Past Angmering and then turning towards the sea at Ferring, I was only about fifteen miles from Brighton now. Along the front at Worthing I looked out to sea where the grey met the grey just offshore. It all looked rather bleak.

Just remember the saying though *"Every cloud has a silver...er... sixpence!"* I needed to brush up on my sayings.

At least, I thought to myself, all the big climbs had gone now until I reached Hastings, unless I made a major faux-pas. I'd conveniently forgotten the bit between Brighton and Eastbourne.

Along the promenade even the seagulls and the pigeons were walking (not together, I add). There was lots of squawking baby seagulls scavenging around the bins.

I don't think that I've ever seen a baby pigeon though, strange!

The road started to move inland again away from the sea as I approached Shoreham-by-sea. I crossed over the bridge on the River Kwai, not really, it was the River Adur (I just wanted to write that cuz I'm a little tinker!), and carried on over a roundabout into the main High Street, passing several places to stock up on supplies, I had no desire to stop yet. I just wanted the rain to stop instead.

I didn't realize that the river continued on my Right (Adur, not Kwai) into the harbour as I couldn't really see the buildings on the far side through the misty rain.

Before long I was pedalling in a more industrial area of the town with Halfords and B&Q on the Left and the elongated harbour on my Right. I quickly reverted to riding on the path again as I passed Lidl and Travis Perkins builders merchants as it felt a lot safer than jousting with the cars, transits and trucks.

Anyway, there weren't any pedestrians about as anybody with just one iota of sense would have been sheltering indoors. Only ducks and old fools on bikes would be stupid enough to be out in this, and I never saw any ducks!

The narrowing path forced me back on the road. Houses now faced the stretched out harbour. I came to a set of traffic lights where the main flow appeared to turn Left but a helpful road worker (another one) told me to keep on going straight. Just as well he did, I thought, as I was going to go with the flow. Why I wanted to turn to the North I don't know. Perhaps it felt strange that I hadn't made a mistake for a while.

As I left him, the chap shouted *"Marmite, 9 inches of it"* I thought *"That's laying it on a bit thick!"* (That didn't really happen, it just made me chuckle).

As I carried on straight, alongside the docks passing a lorry park and warehouses, I really did start to doubt my route.

As I looked out across the water, I'm sure that I spotted through the murk, an Ark containing various pairs of animals. Did that bearded man wave to me from the deck? Perhaps he did but perhaps I'll never Noah!

A cargo freighter *"The Liverpool Princess"* was being unloaded beside some large silo's and other buildings, and now there were some blocks of flats, and sailing boats, that suddenly changed the aspect, although not the colour of the sky which was still battleship grey, just like my old granddads skirting boards and doors that I recalled from my youth.

Why are buildings called buildings when they're already built?

This port seemed to go on forever.

The "Liverpool Princess", I believe Noah's Ark had just sailed behind it!

There was something that I then realized. I was smiling, nay, chuckling to myself. It was wet, it was miserable, I was soaked, Nobby was soaked, my panniers were soaked, the view was debatable, but here I was. I was doing it. Taking the rough with the smooth, and there had been plenty of the rough this day, but it didn't matter.

Remember, you can't make an egg without breaking a few omelettes! I'm just saying.

If it had been sunny, hot and dry with a good following wind all the way with no hills or mistakes it wouldn't have been anywhere near as much of an achievement. I was actually revelling in these conditions. I didn't have any other choice than to be positive.

Walking and even standing without pain at times could be a problem for me, but I could ride a bike, this bike, customised by myself to suit my cycling style and posture, despite being weighed down with all of my gear, and my directional malfunctions from time to time, I was plodding on, unsupported through the rain and I was enjoying every sodden minute of it.

I know that I must have looked a right old sight, at times leaving a bow wave behind me as I steered through another mass of liquid, trying to avoid pot holes that were hard to see under water whilst trying not to swerve out into the path of the massive juggernauts, but I didn't care, I couldn't care, I couldn't think of owt other than enjoying the experience and reaching my next checkpoint that was mapped out in my mind.

Shoreham gradually became Portslade-by-sea, and then I discovered the seafront cycle path at Hove. This was cushty.

The big grey pointy stick in the distance on Brighton seafront

I thought that I'd celebrate by getting a coffee and burger or something at a seafront stall that I'd stopped at.

I perused the menu in the rain for several minutes. Once I had decided on a exceedingly expensive bacon and egg bap and a coffee, I approached the counter, only to be told rather abruptly by the serving chap in a strong Eastern European accent that they were closing.

He had stood there and watched me, whilst I stood in the rain studying the menu board for about five minutes.

It was two minutes shy of midday, for the love of Mike!

It appeared that just because I was their only potential customer in the inclement weather (Slight drizzle to me, Huh!) they were shutting up shop.

I thanked the chap for allowing me to loiter pointlessly around his menu board in the pouring rain with no hope of any service.

 He ignored me.

I lifted Nobby off his stand and, sopping wet, with Nobby's lights still flashing, I pedalled off along the front, looking like *"Torchy The Battery Boy"* in a wet suit!

 Yep, I was really pedalled off!

That was several more minutes of my life that I wasn't getting back.

The other thing that I noticed was that the chap spoke like the character that Del Boy and Rodney brought back from France in *"Only Fools And Horses"* GARY!

That made me smile as I cycled away. I had been looking forward to a lovely balmy summer's day pootling along by the sea but once again…. Hey Ho!

 "Que Sera, Sera", whatever that might mean. All I know is *"What will be, will be"*

So it was onwards to the great metropolis of Brighton. Well, the seafront anyway.

After last year's episode with all of the crowds on the promenade, it was a complete contrast this time with only a few hardy, or foolhardy souls out braving the elements, which were, I have to say easing and starting to clear up a bit.

Some students, adorned in gowns and mortar boards with their proud families in all their finery were pouring across the road from a University to get their photographs taken, trying to blot out the conditions but at the same time, having to hold their mortar boards on their heads.

They were all jolly and were laughing, greatly relieved I expect to receive their degree or whatever it was that they'd strived for. Soon it would be *"Welcome to the real World"* so I don't blame them for enjoying the time and the accolades whilst they could. I felt the same when I was thirteen and I got a *"B+"* in French.

I didn't exactly see the establishment from where they all appeared as I was concentrating on avoiding them as they crossed my path. It could have been the University of Life or Sea World for all I could tell.

At sea, now visible, were the remains of the West Pier, and looming in front of me, with the top half shrouded in mist, was the eyesore (in my humble opinion) of the British Airways i360. A ridiculous (again, only in my opinion) thin, bland concrete tower which can raise folk on a platform about four miles into the sky (I haven't researched this bit).

Today, if it was working and not broken down again, any flight (Yes they call them that) over about one hundred feet would be utterly pointless.

I just can't seem to get my head around the Idea of demolishing old structures, some real things of beauty and heritage, and replacing them with blots on the landscape like this…this…this… stick! An enormous grey, featureless pointy thing on a seafront once bedecked with Victorian architecture. Well, that's progress for you.

The big grey, bland, pointy stick thing doesn't look at all out of place with all of the Victorian street lamps etc. below, does it? Urgh!

I suppose (in fact I know, as my family keep telling me) that I've got my entrenched views as a person, born and bred on a farm deep in the South East Kent countryside in the late fifties/ early sixties. A Proper *"Darling Buds Of May"* country upbringing.

PERFICK!

I've seen the Channel Tunnel, roads and motorways decimate the area, my area, concreting over fields that can never be replaced. My poor girls are always being told by me that things were much better in the fifties, sixties and seventies. I do actually believe that, and yes,

I know that we only remember and dwell on the good bits (It was good though).

I suppose that *"Beauty is in… er .. your chickens before they hatch!"* and all of that old baloney.

I do like a rant from time to time, especially now as I'm growing older (I'll soon be nearly middle aged). The only thing that I don't complain about is my disability and constant pain (Have I mentioned that?).

I've had it for fifty years so I'm just about immune to it. So are my family, they just tell me to get on with it (Bless 'em), so I just get on my bike!

In fact, I wasn't in Gail's good books a while ago. I got her a giant helium balloon for her birthday. That didn't go down very well! (Sorry,again).

Back to my adventure, as I progressed along the front towards the former Palace Pier, now called the Brighton Pier, the posh hotels like the Hilton are being replaced by more seasidey (Is that a word? It is now) shops, cafes, restaurants etc. I found a fish and chip shop where I could sit down, with Nobby parked just outside the open side, next to me. It looked quite a popular place so I ordered two sausages, chips and a cup of tea. I sat and relaxed a bit and ate my lunch.

It was now about 2pm and I had plenty of time to reach my Airbnb at Rottingdean. Poor old Nobby was a bit wet, like me, but at least the saddle was still dry thanks to the plastic bags. The foam handlebar grips were squelchy and the front panniers seemed to be holding up quite well. Some water had got through in a few places but things were mainly dry inside. My back panniers had been covered with my yellow waterproof cover for most of the journey, mainly because it made me more visible than anything else, but it was working.

I finished my food, it was okay but nowt to write home about, and I went to the counter to pay.

"£8.95" said the money grabbing multi millionaire at the till.

After two other diners had picked me up from the floor and slapped me around the face with a wet haddock (£14.50), I asked him to check my bill again, I was sure that He'd mistaken me for someone who'd had a starter, pudding and a bottle of house wine with his dinner.

 He repeated "£8.95 please"

Yes, I Know, I know now. It's "Brighton prices". A few chips, not even one medium sized potato, two basic tasteless sausages which needed ketchup to give them any flavour (He didn't charge me for that) and a normal size cup of tea, not a bucketful, just a cup.

Oh, how I dislike these rip-off places. I'm just a country boy after all, a damp country boy on a heavily laden damp touring bike.

So, light of pocket and heavy of heart as somebody who felt, like a sheep at shearing time, like he'd been fleeced! I re-crossed the road to the cycle path and mooched on. As I climbed up out of Brighton past the marina, I sheltered down behind a wall to give my other half a call. Gail had finished work and was on the bus home. She liked me to check in from time to time during the day so that she could confirm that all was okay with Nobby and me and also to check that we hadn't been abducted or enrolled in any deeply religious commune.

Secretly, I think that she just wanted to be reassured of my directional diligence (meaning, that I wasn't making my way to Penzance or Middlesboro).

I allayed her fears by confirming my location and chosen route. Just keep the sea on my Right, basically.

Onwards I trundled along the cliff top cycle path. I passed the massive Roedean school and then turned Left, away from the A259 into, what I believed to be Rottingdean. A couple of miles down the road to Woodingdean I realized my navigational error as my Airbnb was only meant to be a couple of hundred metres from the main road.

So, that went well!

Back I went to the roundabout, Left (East) and on for another mile or so, and there was Rottingdean High Street. I stopped at a Tesco Express general store at the junction to get some munchies for the evening. A cold pasty, sausage roll, crisps, chocolate and a drink would be my supper again. Where were all of these protein bars and cycle friendly foods that I was supposed to be eating?

Oh, I did buy bananas!

I may not be clever, I may not be bright, but at least I'm stupid…….. Hang on, I think I'm missing a *"not"* there!

My Wednesday night host, Katherine, was delightful and so was her spaniel called Lily. I had to leave Nobby locked up in the back garden this time so I covered him in a large waterproof dust sheet that I had got especially for this reason on the trip. He was well locked to some serious garden furniture as well so he was secure, dry and snug.

I could see him from my bedroom window, and although it was still dampish out, it was warm so I put my trainers on the windowsill to catch the breeze. They wouldn't dry out but it would help a bit.

Well, it would have helped a bit if one of them hadn't fallen into the yard below!

After a welcome cup of brown and a chat and chuckle with Katherine, she took Lily for a walk along the cliffs to chase the herds of seagulls and I went and had a lovely shower and changed into some drier attire. There was even a hairdryer in my room. Oh deep joy!

I did venture downstairs during the evening to make a hot drink and I had another great yarn with Katherine and her brother, then it was back up to my room for my supper (Oh yummy not), a read of my, now, moist book and a call home, followed by a call to Andi to let her know we were still alive.

I have to report that at this point I discovered that my Fitbit watch that they had bought me wasn't working. Actually that's not entirely true. Every time that I had pushed my hand inside my jacket I inadvertently turned it off. This, I didn't discover until I got home. I didn't let on either!

What an intrepid adventurer I was becoming.

13   You can shove your breakfast ...

After a very good night's sleep I was up bright and early. It was nice to put clean dry clothes on and, now, only damp trainers. All bags packed up and back on a slightly wet trusty steed (At least my padded saddle was still dry thanks to the plastic bag), I had a last cuppa with Katherine and Lily, a good luck hug from Katherine and a sloppy lick from Lily (I think that it was that way round) and I was once again on my way.

Breakfast wasn't included in the price as there were plenty of eating establishments along the High Street. I chose to ignore all of them as I was in the saddle and couldn't be bothered to stop.

Once again, not a very good or sensible option as I could have at least stocked up on rolls and pastries for the day. What a dimwit!

At the end of the High Street, it was a Left turn back onto the cycle lane of the A259. It was a fair old climb up the hill and along the cliff top. The cycle lane transferred from the road to the path. Luckily, despite being a rather grey morn, the wind was behind me. HURRAH!

With a lovely view of the white cliff faces ahead on a downhill section, I glided past the Saltdean Lido. Even though it was a gloomy start to the day, I'm sure that I spotted a couple of hardy folk around the pool.

It reminded me of that old saying *"There's nowt so queer as folk...er...playing many a good tune on an old fiddle"*.

Now it was a climb again up to Telscombe cliffs, this time, on the sea side of the road. It felt great to be passing Telscombe stores where last year I'd bought the tastiest bag of salted peanuts that I could remember.

Why didn't I go in and get another bag? Doh!

Soon after the store, I was passing the Wimpy where I had dined near the end of that inglorious failure

"Cooey, Duncan".

I was determined not to fail again, *"Not this time!"* I shouted out to nobody in particular, although an elderly couple did give me a bit of a look.

The track was about 100 metres from the cliffs (Track? That's a bit Aussie), separated by several short roads of assorted houses. I was now riding through Peacehaven.

At a junction I was waved down by two fellow female cycle tourists (I don't mean that I'm a female as well, but they were female, I'm not, no way Pedro, my long golden tresses make me look windswept and interesting, not Girly. The wind doesn't blow that way in my world. And I'll scratch anyone who says otherwise!).

Anyway up, they were heading West, Brighton way, and they had stopped me to ask for directions!

They were asking ME!!!!!

They told me that they had left Seaford that morning. We exchanged route details, me telling them that their route was easy and straightforward, plain sailing (even though they were pedalling into a strong headwind, you don't mention the bad bits to fellow cyclists, never, as it can dishearten them).

They told me that it was murderously hilly between Newhaven and Eastbourne despite me having a following wind, I'd need it!

Ta for that, ladies.

We wished each other *"Bon voyage",* though why we spoke French, I don't know, and then we just passed on, like ships in the night, except that it was morning, and we weren't ships.....and we didn't just pass. But apart from that, that was what it was like.

It was nice to see fellow bike travellers and have an, albeit, brief chat but now it was back to just Nobby and me, all alone but cycling along a recognizable road.

I went to a therapy group to help cope with loneliness once but nobody else turned up!

This was easy…. Until, that is, I came across a new section of cycle path, new since last year. Just as the road took a bend, a cycle sign announced *"Newhaven",* so off I went over a newly Tarmacked path until I found myself on a large housing estate and all of the blue cycle signs had done a runner! Hey Ho!

I cycled round and round like Dougal, Brian, Florence and Zebedee, trying to do three things at once. I tried to look as if I knew where I was going, I tried to look cool and unfazed by the labyrinth of roads on the estate, and I tried to find the damned way out of there!

Eventually though, I had to stop and ask a local builder how to get back onto the Newhaven road. I wasn't actually crying, honestly.

Once he had directed me back to the exact spot where I'd left the road almost half an hour earlier, I continued on my way, thinking that that was another half hour of my life that I wasn't getting back. So much for just following the big highlighted line on my map!

Thankfully the cycle lane stayed on the path until I crossed at the crossing for Pelican cyclists. There was still no sign of any Pelicans on bikes!

I think that the Council have wasted their money there as I can't remember seeing any Pelicans on bikes, or walking, at all on the trip, although I did think that I may have spotting a Penguin on a skateboard in the distance at Fareham!

I really think that I'm starting to lose touch with reality at times!

I pushed Nobby up the steep hill to finally overlook Newhaven harbour.

This was the one part of the trip that I had genuine problems with.

I don't mean this one particular hill, but any time that I had to dismount and push as it was very awkward and painful. All that I could do was to lean on good old Nobby as much as I could and shuffle along using him as a kind of crutch or stick. I bet it looked a right old sight.

I knew that this would be the case prior to doing any of this and the alternative was to do nowt. And, by eck, I was enjoying myself, even on the uphill hard bits. Any hard slog up a hill, and there were plenty, was followed by me staggering back onto the saddle and getting some motion going again, in both, the wheels and in my joints, and freewheeling downhill can't be beaten.

WHEEEEEEEE!!!!

Down the hill through the large estate I went, not needing to pedal at all until I reached the port. I skirted around the River Ouse, across the bridge beside the port entrance and railway station, past my pick up point from the previous year (A very despondent moment then, but a much different, better feeling today) and back along the main road towards Seaford, only three miles further on.

I was now riding back on the carriageway as I climbed steadily uphill, keeping as close to the road edge as I could. My progress was about as quick as an overweight hippo reversing up an alley but then... a cycle path on the opposite side of the road.

A rapid-ish dismount and limp across and I found myself now separated from the main highway by a verge and bushes. In fact, in places the road vanished completely from view. A purpose built path for walkers and cyclists which made the uphill gradient feel so much easier.

Again, it's this thing of not knowing what's around the corner, over the hill, on the other side of the road, of not knowing where anything is. It's what it's all about (Not the Hokey Cokey), everything is new and unseen before. Each and every single turn of the pedals is part of the adventure. Ooh, it's so hard to explain, but I'm trying! (I'm very trying, some might say).

The *"Welcome to Seaford"* sign claimed it to be a Cinque Port from 1229-1883. I couldn't figure that out as my home town, Hythe, is a Cinque Port along with Hastings, Dover, Sandwich and Rye (it was formerly New Romney), Cinque, as in, Five.

Seaford was one of several *"Limbs"* of Hastings. So there! Don't push it, Seaford.

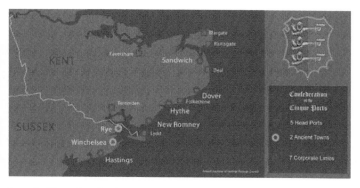

Map showing Kent and Sussex with towns including Margate, Ramsgate, Sandwich, Deal, Dover, Folkestone, Hythe, New Romney, Lydd, Rye, Winchelsea, Hastings, Faversham, and Tenterden. Confederation of the Cinque Ports: 5 Head Ports, 2 Ancient Towns, 7 Corporate Limbs.

I know that it's an old map but this is what I've been brought up to believe as fact and there is nobody alive from that period to prove me wrong, so there!

And there endeth my own totally unbiased local history lesson.

It's weird what you think about when you're cycling, at least I haven't come up with any stupid sayings or owt lately.

Still, it's best not to put all of your eggs in ..er.. one chicken!

Sorry about that one, I couldn't resist. Still, it's better to be hung for a sheep than a porpoise!

The road (remember the road?) finally levelled out as the path rejoined it and the houses disappeared. The day was brightening up, the sun was finally making a welcome re-appearance after almost two days off.

All of a sudden I was climbing again on a narrower path facing oncoming traffic. It was much steeper this time, turning the upward side into two lanes so I was grateful to be where I was. In a gap in the hill I could see the English Channel. As I passed through the town I realised that I was quite a bit higher up than the shoreline.

I could see the edges of cliffs in the distance. I had a decision to make.

Do I take a high path or roadway (I wasn't sure what it was) up and over the Seven Sisters South Downs Way to Birling Gap and, finally, to Beachy Head along the cliff tops with several big climbs and probable stunning views or do I stick to the main route through to Eastbourne via Friston and East Dean?

So as I headed onwards along the A259 towards Eastbourne, via Friston and East Dean, with some glimpses down side roads to the cliffs, I truly thought what a pleasant section of road this was. At the time it wasn't too busy at all and I felt that hopefully now it would be downhill to Eastbourne seafront where I would treat myself to a nice lunch.

Things felt really good, Nobby was performing like poetry in motion, almost gliding along. His wheels purring as I turned the pedals effortlessly without even thinking about what I was doing.

I felt as chipper as chippy the chipbird in a very chipper situation, then, as I left the Seaford town limits (Still claiming former Cinque Ports status, yeah right!) I was faced with open countryside with views for miles ahead with cliffs and sea to the Right of me.

The road ahead looked like it was as undulating as the A360 to Salisbury, only probably more so. Any path had now disappeared completely so I was now competing for space on a narrow two lane main road with cars, lorry's, coaches, buses, motorhomes, caravans, motorbikes, vans and low flying second world war bombers (I may have made the last one up).

But what a view!!!!

I could clearly see the Cuckmere River winding down to Cuckmere Haven where it spilled into the sea. I pedalled down to the bridge that spanned the river and enjoyed a glorious vista of the river in both directions.

The knowledge that I was now at sea level registered very quickly as I anticipated a possible gradient back upwards again. At least there was a path to use again.

Eastbourne was now only six miles away according to the road sign.

The climb became too severe (for me) and I was forced off Nobby for a long crippling push up a long straight section. These are both good and bad (in a bad sort of way). Good, because the traffic can clearly see you as they approach, this gives them even more time to get the hump with you as you've slowed down their progress, and bad, because you can't ever seem to reach the end.

There was nowhere to pull over and rest. I had to climb up onto the verge on a few occasions as this hill was a bit of a killer for me.

What was that I said about feeling chipper?

There were some less severe bits where, after getting my legs back from their jellified state, I was able to pedal, albeit in a very low gear, culminating with the Granny gear coming into operation for the umpteenth time.

After what seemed like two weeks and several further heart attacks, but was actually nearer an hour, I reached what was the summit (I hoped). This felt like the longest, hardest actual climb of the journey so far.

My little ticker was pounding away at many thousand beats per minute (or so it felt). I knew from experience that this was fine though, all I needed to do was to just have a little rest, take some water on board and gently push on once my heart rate was back near normal.

It was amazing to think how far my emotions, fears and knowledge had come from the early days after my heart attack. Exercise helps towards a healthy heart, and, by Golly, you do feel good about yourself when you've done something positive and active to help yourself.

If I'm feeling a bit down for any painful reason on my bike, I always try to remember that there are folk that would love to be able to do what I'm doing, but can't.

I haven't tried to hide from my failures, that's why I've written about them, but my willpower, pride, determination and desire got stronger and stronger as I went, and then there was the enjoyment, followed by my own very personal minor sense of achievement.

All of these silly little bits helped to drive me on, and I'm nowt special. You've probably already noticed that.

But I was enjoying myself!

At Friston it got back to just minor undulations, except for one place where I descended a 16% hill. This partly made up for the terrible climb that I'd just endured.

Even during this downhill section I was still holding up the traffic, even though I must have been doing up to 25mph. I was only guessing of course, as my bike computer was waterlogged and kaput. Perhaps I was doing 65mph!

Okay, my first guess was much nearer.

It didn't make no never mind to me though as I was determined to hold my line away from the edge of the road, and also away from any possible potholes. Once the hill levelled out I managed to find the footpath for a bit to allow the motorists through. I always hold up my hand to say thank you to any people stuck behind me. I've found that if you're courteous, most folk are courteous back.

I did say most folk. Some drivers can still be rude or abusive, but then again, so can some cyclists.

Just remember, *"Do unto others as they.. er.. cry over spilt milk"*.

Always remember that and you won't go far wrong.

The path ended all too soon, just as another steady climb started. This must have lasted over a mile, although it felt like ten, but at the top I could look over to the Right and see the sea in the distance.

I hadn't realized how far from the coast the road had taken me. I was right up on the South Downs now and Beachy Head was only two miles away on the B2103.

On a whim I took the turning. It was brilliant being up on this high road, as the road fell I could see Eastbourne and its pier slightly in front and to the Left.

I was fairly flying down this section of the B2103, surrounded by touristy traffic, and I left it too late to brake, signal and turn Right to gain a view over the famed Lighthouse.

 There was no way that I could now stop and cycle back up the hill so I kept on going down the 12% gradient and I even missed a turn off for the seafront, so I carried on down towards the town centre.

I was still quite a bit above the town when, due entirely to my uncanny sense of direction, or more truthfully, due totally to pot luck, I took a couple of turns based on absolutely no knowledge whatsoever, and I found myself overlooking the English Channel.

It's a piece of cake, this navigation lark!

I then confidently cycled eastwards towards the pier. It all looked quite posh, with a Victorian air, only spoilt by all of the modern cars parked along Grand Parade.

The public gardens along the front were all in bloom, showing off the area in the best possible way. As I reached the pier it became impossible to do anything other than push Nobby through the blue rinsed throng of so many elderly ladies (and a few gents, but none with a blue rinse).

They were all pouring out of the numerous coaches, all parked near the pier entrance, either on day trips or just arriving at hotels nearby. Their moods seemed to match the mood of the day now, sunny and bright.

I can't recall seeing one miserable or unhappy person amongst this jolly band of senior citizens, as they made their way either to, or from their respective buses. I expect that, like myself, many had looked forward to their excursion for a long time.

As I passed by the pier, I couldn't find anywhere to buy food so I backtracked, back through the happy throng of wibbly wobbly old ladies (and men, although there did seem to be far more ladies) and onto Terminus Road, which looked like it had several eateries.

I'd only travelled a short distance down the road when I spotted, on my Left, a menu board showing a full all day breakfast. There were plenty of empty outside tables so, with lips being licked, I parked Nobby on his stand close to me but out of anyone's way and then sat at a table, ready to order some well deserved food when, from deep within the bowels of the near empty restaurant, came a Whirling Dervish of a man who shouted at me from a snarled up face that could curdle milk, that I would have to move Nobby into a cycle rack as he was blocking the entrance for his customers.

I looked around me, totally bemused. Surely this impolite excuse for a human being couldn't have been addressing me? Could he?

He had the temperament and facial expression of an old man who had been constipated for several days!

"You vill 'ave to move eet!" he shouted in an accent that I didn't take to be local. *"Pardon?"* I replied as I stood up and gestured around with my arm. *"What customers? What entrance? It's not obstructing owt"*

With that, I told him where I thought his all day breakfast may be better suited, flicked Nobby from his stand and walked away feeling, despite a still empty stomach, so much better.

"Well Nobby, my old mate, he made us about as welcome as a fart in an astronaut's suit!" Nobby nodded in agreement (In my mind).

I'd only pushed a few metres along when I found myself at the Odyssey Fish & Chip Restaurant. They had outside tables in the sunshine. Deep joy!

I locked my mate to a chair, wandered in and ordered a cheeseburger, salad and chips and a can of cola (you guess which brand).

The complete contrast in attitude and friendliness of the staff was like comparing night and day. I stood and chatted to the chap at the front while my food was being prepared, and when it arrived it was massive, and it was also the best cheeseburger, salad and chips that I could remember eating. It was so good, I took a picture of it (obviously before I'd eaten it). What a sad little person I was becoming!

Please don't judge me as a food critic or as a person!

This was just the bit of respite and rejuvenation that I needed. The young chap couldn't imagine how his friendliness and interest (genuine, I believe) in my trip had given me a boost.

After my meal, they even stood guard over Nobby for me so that I could use the loo at the back of the restaurant, then they gave me some good advice on the next part of my route.

And, no, it wasn't *"Catch the train"*.

Such nice people, and I would wholeheartedly recommend this establishment to any other weary cyclist or traveller. Obviously the same could not be said for the other place with Mr. Grumpy Gitface! I bet his eggs were all runny as well.

Back up to Grand Parade I went and past the pier and the *"Granny's on tour"* coaches and buses, and onward.

I know that they call Eastbourne *"God's waiting room"* but there looked to be plenty of life and fun in most of the older folk there. Perhaps it was the sun, perhaps it was the sea air, but perhaps it was because they weren't on a bike!

A typical? Eastbourne summer beach scene with hardly any room to swing a cat (although folk were swinging them just out of shot)

It was mainly hotels now along the front, and it was a glorious afternoon with any slight wind or breeze at my back. The road drifted away from the seawall, I'm sure that I could have stayed on the front for a fair way but my new found friend had advised me to go this way, so I did.

I cycled past the Redoubt fortress of Eastbourne, I was never too far from the beach. I even felt safe now on the road. Life was certainly feeling good this afternoon. This was just as I'd envisaged this part of the journey.

I found the cycle path alongside the road on the way to Pevensey Bay. Ooops! That didn't last long, back on the road again. It was only a couple of miles to Pevensey and it was as flat as a badger's eyebrow! (Don't ask).

I crossed a roundabout and missed a chance to stock up at a supermarket for tonight's snacks. I would regret that later, no doubt.

Cycle path again, jolly good show. As I've said before, any chance to get away from the traffic is a bonus as long as you respect other users of the path or track.

I seemed to be doing a lot of singing to myself today. Maybe it was because, at last, I knew that I was going to do it.

No, it wasn't, Not yet, I wouldn't, couldn't, let myself think that, as lots of things could still conspire against me.

I think that it was just because I was having a good day in the saddle, despite the hills of earlier.

I only had about thirteen miles left to do today to my Airbnb at St. Leonards. At Pevensey I asked an elderly lady (I seemed to be seeing lots of those today) if the road straight across from some traffic lights was the road to Norman's Bay. She said that she thought it was, then she scuttled off rather quickly so that I couldn't ask her owt else.

I was only going to ask her what street did the old woman who lived in a shoe, live in? Perhaps she thought that I appeared crazy after being out in the sun almost all day.

I think that sometimes you get to think too much when you're turning the pedals, meandering along. Earlier I had spent several minutes wondering who washed up at the last supper.

Does anybody know what Geronimo shouts as he jumps out of a plane?

And this is after only a few days!

The coast road carried on with, at first houses, then bungalows and static *Mobile* homes (How Does that work?).

All of a sudden it appeared that I'd run out of public highway and was possibly on some sort of private road. This was where all of the campsites were, the ones that I had marked off as possible night stops last year, but never made it.

Too be honest, they all looked really nice. The sort of place where I could have lost my *"Tenting virginity"* (Is *"Tenting"* a real word?), who knows? Who cares?

There was a little railway crossing at Norman's Bay station. It was no more than a platform really. Once I had crossed, I was back on the main public road or *"Sluice Lane"* as it was romantically called. There was actually a pub here called the Star Inn, almost in the middle of nowhere.

I could imagine many an inebriated driver zigzagging their way back to the campsites at night along the pitch dark lane!

Black sky at night, night.

Back sky in the morning... er.... Still night!

Onwards I travelled along the windy lane (that's *"Windy"* as in, *"It winds round a corner"* and not *"Windy"* as in *"Windy Miller"*), I thought that it was important to mention that, perhaps not.

The lane then re-crossed the rail line. I'd worked it out that it must be the Coastal line between Eastbourne and Hastings. Straight after the crossing I came to the seawall. I parked up Nobby, climbed the steps to admire the windswept view back towards Eastbourne and on to Hastings in the East.

It was great to have a break here, just to sit, take some pictures and have a drink. I even got to see a train passing by, the one for the

week, perhaps.

Looking East from the beach

Looking West from the beach

I knew a man who always wanted to be run over by a steam train, and when it happened he was chuffed to bits! (I promise I'll stop, honest).

I looked down at my laden bike and actually said to myself out loud *"I am a touring cyclist"*

There wasn't anybody else there, that's why I had a wee as well!

There was a golf course on the other side of the track but there was nobody on it.

Looking down at my mate (Pre wee wee. Er.. I mean Pre comfort break) (for a wee wee!)

I got Back on board and I pootled along, not in any hurry, just taking in the sea air and staring out, over towards France. Gliding between parked cars and camper vans, it almost felt as if I was on *"home turf"* with just a shingle beach separating me from the water.

There were beach huts and a few seaside houses now on my Right, the railway line was on my Left and Nobby and me cruising along the narrow lane in between.

I passed Cooden Beach Station and took a Right turn onto Cooden Drive and into a slight rise. This area had quite an air of poshness about it, although I expect that we lowered the tone a fair bit as we ambled through, with me singing and Nobby nodding his handlebars to the beat!

Another Right turn (all done by complete guesswork, I might add) and I was on a promenade above the pebbly beach. This part of the coast at Bexhill was grand. I had been to Bexhill many years previous, to a much less salubrious area (snobby little snob) and I wasn't even aware that owt like this existed here.

Time for an ice lolly along Bexhill or St. Leonards seafront. I was confused!

The sun was beating down now and despite the quite strong tailwind, I felt that it was time for a break. I was definitely on the seafront now, with blocks of flats gazing straight out to sea, with not a jot, or a blot on the prom to spoil or impede their view, and what a view to wake up to!

No big grey concrete stick here! Take note Brighton!

I pulled up at a fish & chips, Ice cream, Tea shop (Woah there Nobby!), and indulged myself in a strawberry mivvi type lolly (Remember those?). Well, I can honestly say that they don't taste as they used to, but I still sat at an outside table slurping away, and then I followed that up with a coffee as I watched the waves roll in up the beach.

I was feeling content as I knew that I wasn't more than a couple of miles or so from my Airbnb (Although I didn't take into account that I may cycle around in circles for a while as I lost my bearings once I left the seafront!).

At the De La Warr Pavilion I turned up into the town centre to acquire some food for the evening. I stopped at the Co op and asked the manager if I could lock Nobby up in a large area just inside the shop near the tills as I didn't want to lose him or anything off him now.

The manager very kindly gave his consent so I parked and locked him and jokingly said to the girl on the till "*I'll leave you in charge of my bike!*"

she just glared at me and spat "*Not my problem!*", I just smiled at her and wandered off to do my shopping, not feeling as confident as I was regarding Nobby's safety.

I was back at his side inside five minutes with just a small packet of biscuits and a cokey type drink. I wasn't leaving my buddy anywhere near "*Little Miss Sulky Drawers*" as I now like to think of her.

I made my way back to the seafront and locked Nobby in the doorway of a small Mace corner shop, went in and bought some crisps, nuts and a pasty. I certainly knew how to live it up. I then tried to cut up through the town to relocate the A259 main road.

This was where I lost my bearings completely and ended up riding round and round for a while until I did eventually chance upon it.

It's at this point that I think a confession may be in order.

It wasn't until many weeks later that I actually realized that I was still in Bexhill-on-sea. At the time I honestly thought that I was in St. Leonards, even the names on some shops (e.g. *"Bexhill Age UK"*) and the railway station name *"BEXHILL"* didn't register at all with me.

That's how bad my navigational talents apparently were, and despite my description and alleged knowledge of my location that I have just tried to convey, I was, in fact, a geographical charlatan in that instance.

I'm so glad to relieve myself of the guilt of my deception. There, now you have it!

I was so inept in my adventure that, and not for the first time, I was actually describing sights in a completely different town from the one that I was convinced that I'd arrived in!

Hey Ho! Please don't judge me on my geographical knowledge (or lack of it).

Anyway, it didn't make no never mind to the journey as I located my night's resting place within half an hour or so, so Ne Ne Ne Ne Ne!

My host for the night had the delectable name of Gigi!

It's a name to conjure up thoughts of Parisienne nights, the Champs Elysees, the Eiffel Tower and Moulin Rouge.

In fact he was a bricklayer, whose real name was Geoff!

Gigi or Geoff ! Not really folks.

Only joshing. She was actually a delightful, warm lady with a lovely welcoming homely abode.

After I was shown to my room which had a view of the sea, which wasn't too far away, I had a well earned shower and sorted my gear out. Nobby was parked on the patio, to be moved into the dining room during the evening.

I ventured downstairs to make myself a cup of brown and spent some time, hopefully, entertaining my host, Gigi, and a fellow Airbnb user, a young Australian girl (see, another Aussie) with my travel tales of the past few days. When I thought that they had heard enough of my yarns (or were bored witless) I took my leave and headed back upstairs to partake in my culinary delight of supper.

I phoned Andi for my evening check in, and called home to Gail and Jodie to regale them all of the details of the day. Gail asked me when I roughly expected to be home the next day. Obviously (in my mind) they were planning a large welcoming committee with flags and bunting, and even possibly, a civic reception to greet their intrepid conquering hero, although they never said!

14   Homeward Bound

After a restful night, I was up and about early yet again and after a quick cup of tea with Gigi, who was off to point a wall! (Not really, sorry Geoff, I mean Gigi), I was loaded up and off along Hastings seafront.

The town was yet to come alive as it was only seven fifteen. It was a dull overcast day with rain looking likely but at least the wind was still at my back. This was promising to be a short day as I only had around forty odd miles to do.

After buying a sandwich for later at a garage and nibbling on an oat bar for breakfast, I was faced with a gradual climb up and out of the town. Well, the gradient wasn't too bad at first but then it got harder and harder and harder (I hope that I've emphasized just how hard it had got!).

 It took a fair bit of time to reach the turn off for Fairlight, with at least three stops to admire no view at all (I was just out of power), and most of the ascent was completed on the footpath as I was going so slow a tortoise with a heavy briefcase overtook me on his way to work, and it was now quite a busy road.

The road up to Fairlight seemed to be just as steep, if not worse, with a continuous climb with no let up or path to hide on this time. At least the traffic was lighter on this road with only two mobility scooters and a steam roller edging to get past.

I knew that this was going to be a difficult part of the journey before I had started, but I also knew that once it had been conquered it was all downhill and then flat across the marsh to the finish.

I didn't feel like I had muscles anymore, only pain. Was I dragging a bike now made out of lead?

I was shouting to myself again, things like *"C'mon wee man , keep going, just a wee bit more"* and other less printable comments, apparently, in a Scottish accent that I'd just developed *"See you, Jimmy!"* when…… the road levelled out.

I'm sure that I heard Nobby give out a little whimper (although it could easily have been me) then, after a short stretch when I just kept the pedals turning at a steady 8mph, there was a 12% downhill!

Oh, thank St. Tarmacadam, the patron saint of roads! (I haven't checked that fact).

I didn't even mind the overcast sky that made for an unimpressive vista, nor did I mind the hedgehog on roller skates that passed me! (I'm losing it big time now).

A bit further on, there were slight undulations and then a 10% down to Fairlight. It then flattened out towards Pett and Winchelsea (this was where I overtook the hedgehog as he'd stopped for a ciggie! Apparently, he hadn't seen any of the adverts telling us how bad they were for us as he didn't own a TV!).

Please shoot me now!

There were glimpses of the sea to my Right. The winding road (and, by eck, did it wind?) carried me forth, through Pett Level and alongside the seawall where, at some point, I passed what was left of the Royal Military Canal, my canal, the canal that I'd known and lived alongside all of my life (Although, not this bit).

Cutting away from the sea I passed Rye Bay Caravan Park, quite a large acreage covered by little plastic boxes, housing happy or humpy holidaymakers. I expect that most are a bit of both during their stay.

Winchelsea beach where the road leaves the sea (Nearly home)

Onwards I pedalled, past Winchelsea Sands Holiday Park and on to the A259 junction. A Right turn and over the Royal Military Canal, and on to Rye.

This was very busy but luckily there was a path on the Right side. It was a bit hairy at times when the larger vehicles hammered past me, but it was preferable to being out there with them. The path was very narrow and a laden Nobby was quite wide.

Despite the narrowness, I had to keep moving. *"He who hesitates..er... last.. um..laughs loudest!".*

Soon I had reached Rye and crossed the River Rother (I was cycling over the bridge. I didn't wade through the silty mud).

There were a few wet drops now falling from a leaden sky so I decided to stop at the park and I took shelter beside the public conveniences to eat my sandwich and any other bits that I had left in my bags. I'd dined in better places (and also in a lot worse, I may add).

I got into conversation with a couple of sheltering walkers who were surprised to hear of my trek, and to learn of how near I now was to home, a raucous welcome and celebration, and my own bed.

The bit after *"to home"* in the last paragraph was, to be honest, only played out in my mind and not actually said, but, we'll see.

Whilst parked adjacent to the Gents toilet, I managed to make each person entering feel totally at ease with a cheery *"Morning!"* whilst in no way appearing to look like a pervy weirdo, loitering outside a toilet block!

You can't buy politeness, nor class!

After a few decidedly dodgy looks, I thought it may have been a better Idea to brave the elements, so off I dripped, to meet the main road again at the bridge over the River Kw…. No, I'd done that one, Rother. That was it.

Immediately after crossing the river (the tide was out and it was still mainly silty mud), the cycle path veered off Right, through a gate and along a rough track over the fields. I followed this track through, now, driving rain which was smacking into me from the side, until I reappeared back into some form of civilization at a lay by on the Camber Road.

I only had to cross the road to carry on along a separate specially constructed cinder type track that was apart from the road. I thought that now it should all be plain sailing with a good tailwind and the end almost in sight. I wouldn't be thwarted now.

If Nobby suddenly melted I could still call Jodes to bring my mountain bike, Eric (Yes, they both have names, of course) out to me so that I could still cycle the complete distance. Nobby wouldn't melt though, he was made of sterner stuff and would finish with me.

And then I got a puncture!!!!

Not in the front tyre, oh no, that would be too easy. It was in the back tyre yet again. *"Dash and Blow it"* I think I hollered this time, although I may have shouted something else!

It had happened just when I was several feet away from the road, out of sight behind some, just trimmed, Hawthorn bushes...... Ah, now that may have explained it. There I was, merrily pedalling away, at some miles per hour, admiring gravel pits and a golf course on my Right and the wind turbines on my Left (I had seen these in the Westerly distance on my local jaunts out), when my momentum came to an abrupt halt.

Who plants Hawthorn bushes next to a cycle path? Unbelievable!

Who puts a cycle path next to planted Hawthorn bushes? Double Unbelievable!

The "offending" cycle path near the Kent & Sussex border

Hey Ho! Off came all of the panniers so that I could turn Nobby onto his head, off came the wheel, off came the tyre, out came the flat tube and on went my only other new one. I checked the tyre (I'm not a fool), removed a thorn, and then went through the same procedure, only this time in reverse, and with care.

Still, worse things happen at sea I suppose, although you wouldn't find many Hawthorn bushes out there, nor would you be riding a bike, so, a pointless statement really.

Once all was loaded up I decided to take my chance on the road, despite having the option of the cycle path, I'd lost confidence in my luck regarding the collection of even more thorns. If it happened again I would have to physically repair the puncture. I was unwilling to tempt fate, so it was the road for me.

I made very good time out in the open and fairly flew through Camber, passing Pontins and all of its *"Happy campers"*.

"Hi De Hi" I inwardly chanted as I didn't want to upset or offend any of the inmates... er ... I mean holiday makers. It was the fictional *"Maplins"* and their yellow coats and not Pontins anyway so the comparison ends, unless there's a chalet maid here in Camber called *"Peggy Olleringshaw"* Hi De Hi!

I was riding along the seawall again now, with caravans and tents on my Left, the wind turbines or windmills, as I call them, still alongside, spinning around in the South Westerly breeze. The rain was more drizzly now but my spirits were soaring and I had started singing to myself, not for the first time on the trip, but now with more gusto!

There was a bleak section of seawall with some chalet or pre-fab type dwellings beside the road, just like the familiar ones at Dungeness, a bit further on. In fact, as the road split away from the sea I could see the electricity pylons that run from the power station over the Romney Marsh, up and over the Downs and away to the civilized world beyond.

Us Marsh dwellers like to class ourselves apart as, I believe numerous regions do. I know that the foresters in the Royal Forest of Dean are very protective and proud of their area, and rightly so.

We have a brilliant and unique breed of folk in these parts, people like my old granddad, the man I lived with for several years, born and bred here, like myself (Although I was actually born at Court At Street on a farm, overlooking the marsh. Still, let's not be picky!).

My granddad was my best mate and my hero. Also, the sea air must be pretty good here, as well as the shrimps he used to catch, because he lived to the grand old age of 99 years. As I say, my hero!

I digress, sorry about that (I sound like Ronnie Corbett now). I passed Lydd Ranges on this open windswept section of road. I wouldn't have fancied cycling West into the breeze. A couple of gravel lorry's passed me and gave me a friendly (I hope) toot as they went because I waved them through as soon as it was safe to do so.

I reached Lydd, or as I called it, forty five degrees, as all of the trees appeared to be bent at that angle. I was definitely on home turf now as I pedalled past my cousin, Steve's house, shame he was at work as a cuppa would have been nice.

I had decided to go this way and not down to Dungeness Point and along the seafront all of the way as there would have been a strong crosswind for a while, and at least going this way it's on my back.

I went up and over the railway line, past what is left of the old Lydd station and onwards to New Romney. Although this was my old stomping ground, I had never actually cycled along this particular road. I'd always kept out in the marsh on the country lanes when I could.

Past Lydd Airport and Golf club I went, to meet up with the A259 again before entering New Romney. From there, I cycled along the path and road to St. Marys Bay, where I crossed over onto the seawall. I knew this bit very well as I'd ridden along it many, many times.

I mooched through Dymchurch, on the seawall, past the funfair and carried on to the Redoubt corner where the seawall gave way to Hythe Ranges. There were only two miles left for me to pedal and *"Complete the circle"* as it were (although it wasn't really a circle, just a wonky line).

I was singing Simon & Garfunkel's *"Homeward Bound"* and I was definitely giving it *"The whole nine yards"*, so to speak (or sing).

As I passed the Botolph's Bridge road turning and the old Nicholl's quarry, I felt so chuffed and just a little bit proud of myself.

In my head I could almost hear the Town Brass Band tuning up. *"I do hope that the crowd give me a bit of space to cycle down the Avenue"* I thought as I turned off the A259 for the final time.

Oh!

Not a Dicky Bird!

Not a Bleeding Sausage!

No Bunting!

No Flags!

No Band!

No People!

Not even a dog walker!

Hey Ho! Such is life.

Hang on. What about at the house?

Nope!

If anyone was there, they were hiding very well!

Not even Ralph the cat could be bothered to be there for my triumphant return, and I fed him!

Oh well!

I unlocked the side door, lifted Nobby in, gave him an affectionate pat and thanked him for getting me home. He never let me down once. He couldn't help the punctures, I steered him over those (not intentionally).

I unloaded my panniers, put the kettle on and went and had a shower. It was good to be home, especially as I had finally, successfully completed my little tour.

It was early afternoon when I got home. I finished my cup of brown and walked (or limped) up to the end of the road to meet Gail off the bus. It was a happy reunion. She did actually appear pleased to see me.

My first words were *"I did it"*

"Finally" she replied.

Epilogue

So that was it.

I'd left Gloucester to cycle home, via Wales on Sunday and I'd made it home on the sixth day, Friday.

I'd pedalled (and pushed) just over 320 miles, due to my navigational skills and detours.

In the vast world of cycle touring, it wasn't a major achievement. Some, or many, may argue that it wasn't even a minor achievement. But to me, a long haired, fifty nine year old, disabled, ageing hippy with hardly any actual sense of direction, I think that I did okay.

It may have taken three attempts, but if I achieve little else as a touring cyclist, at least I have this tiny success to look back on.

I suppose that, if nothing else, it should show that anybody with even a modicum of fitness could achieve the same, similar or more (much more).

I learned not to let my disability be an excuse, but instead I made it a major part of the reason for doing it, also, fourteen years ago, lying in a hospital bed after my heart thingy, I couldn't picture a future where anything such as my quest would have featured.

I have tried to write this the same way that I try to live, by being me. It's always better to make folk smile, if possible, or to make them laugh, that's even better.

I apologize if I haven't been serious enough at times, but that's just not me I'm afraid.

As the saying goes *"You can't teach an old dog.. er.. to suck eggs"*

Everything in the book is the truth, it did actually happen, all of my failures and my one final minor success.

There have been no omissions at all (apart from the one about what Jodie did in a small wood when they collected me after my first failure, I promised her that I wouldn't mention that and I'd like to think that I'd kept that promise).

I tried to regale Ralph with tales of my epic adventure but he just pretended to be hypnotized and just ignored me. Hey Ho!

I hope that I have entertained you with my inane drivel. Just bear in mind that my family have to endure it all of the time. For that, to them I apologize.

Not really. Har De Har!

If, by chance, there is anyone reading this who has endured similar or has a disability where cycling could help recovery, then go for it.

Remember *"Tough times don't last, Tough folk do!"* Now that I've got the bug, where to next, I wonder?

I know, I'll just follow the map!

The end.

Printed in Great Britain
by Amazon